1000 REAS
TO PRAISE THE LORD

Johnson Folorunso Ajayi

**Kingdom
Publishers**

1000 Reasons to Praise the Lord
A Gynaecologist lists 1,670 medical and biblical reasons
to thank God with 60 stories.
Copyright© Johnson Folorunso AJAYI

All Scripture Quotations have been taken from the New International Version and
the King James Version of the Bible.

ISBN: 978-1-911697-21-3

1st Edition by Kingdom Publishers

Kingdom Publishers
London, UK.

You can purchase copies of this book from any leading bookstore or
email **contact@kingdompublishers.co.uk**

Dedication

I would like to thank everybody who has encouraged me to write the books I had been promising for quite some time. They are too numerous to mention, and I am likely to miss notable names if I try. Hopefully, this is not the last.

I thank Steve Whittall, who proofread the first draft of this book and made valuable suggestions and Pastor Malcolm Hathaway who wrote the foreword. Thanks too to my wife, Bisi, children Tope, Tomi and Tolu, my brothers, sister, cousins, friends, and classmates at the university who never tired of complimenting my potential and encouraging me to 'put pen to paper' and stop dreaming. After all, the first step in actualizing a dream is to wake up from slumber!

This is my first step, and to God be the glory.

Foreword

We shouldn't be giving reasons to praise God. They are everywhere. Yet, we can become so overwhelmed by the struggles of life that we fail to see the countless blessings God pours on us. How wonderful then to read a book that is devoted to numbering them! Who better to do this than one who dedicated his life not just to Medicine but to caring for mothers and bringing thousands of lives safely into the world. One who has undoubtedly seen more than most!

Johnson's book is a veritable encyclopedia of reasons to praise God. A treasure trove of stories and lessons learned through life's experiences and a lifetime of service as a doctor and Obstetrician-Gynaecologist. A rich compendium of real-life stories and some personal confessions! All seasoned with Johnson's unique African-Nigerian history and perspective. Truly refreshing, uplifting, inspiring, motivating, empowering.

It was my great privilege to know Johnson personally as a member of the Elim Church, Southport, where I served as senior minister for nine years. I came to know him as a true Christian gentleman with an exemplary record as a consultant and surgeon. I heartily commend this book to you. It will lift your spirit and encourage *you* to praise the Lord!

Rev Malcolm Hathaway, BD (London)
June 2021

Contents

List of Short Stories and Explanations

INTRODUCTION

"Praise Be," "Thank God," "Thank Goodness," "The Man up there," "Mother nature is kind," "Fate, Lucky and Fortunate" are some of the ways that we express thanks to the Almighty. After an act of benevolence to a child who turns and walks away, parents usually call the child back to ask, *"And what do you say?"* to which the automatic answer is *"Thank you."* In other words, we teach our children at an early age the understanding and skill to express gratitude for the blessings we receive from people.

The British are reputed to be perhaps the politest of races. You visit the post office, buy stamps and hand your letter over at the counter. The postmaster actually thanks you! He is serving you, and *you* should be doing the thanking. Elsewhere airline staff thank passengers as they step off planes because they had used their services, kept their business going and kept many staff employed.

This fact was missing on a young lady in 1981. I was working in a hospital in Akure where my uncle, who had just arrived by air from the United Kingdom on holiday, came to visit me. He recounted his encounter with an employee of the now-defunct Nigeria Airways who was being contumelious while attending to him at the airport. Comparing her attitude to her British counterparts', he asked her, "Do you know you could lose your job if I stopped flying your airline?" The girl laughed because she could not connect between an ordinary man flying in an economy seat and her job security with the Ministry of Aviation. He stopped patronizing that airline – as did many others because of rather sloppy performances. Today, there is no airline of that cognomen anywhere in the world. The carrier ceased operations in 2003 with debts of over US$528 million despite an attempted bailout by the state.

Jesus Christ used a parable to illustrate that an attitude of gratitude is pleasing to God. Ten lepers had been healed. Leprosy was a cruel disease that caused sufferers in society to live outside city walls. Rabbinic priests did not touch them otherwise, they would be ceremonially unclean. Therefore, being healed was more than being rid of disease: it meant reintegration into society. Anyone would have thought that whoever was healed of that infirmity would rush back to thank the healer. However, only one came back to express gratitude to Jesus. He told this parable because, while not compulsory, appreciation for a favour is commendable.

Various hymn writers encouraged believers to express thanks to God. Charles Wesley wished for a thousand tongues to praise his Redeemer. Isaac Watts invited us to come and join our cheerful songs of praise with angels around the throne of God. Fanny Crosby implored us to sing and proclaim God's tremendous Love in *Praise Him, praise Him, Jesus our blessed Redeemer.*

Although the title states 'one thousand (1000) reasons to praise the Lord,' this book actually lists 1,670 reasons for which we can praise the Lord. There are 60 stories with notes that are added to explain why some of these reasons, which might be overlooked or considered trivial, are good reasons to thank God.

PREFACE

Bay 4 bed 3 was my home for four nights. Four nights that taught me what Medicine did not in my previous forty-one years as a doctor and six as a medical student. I was a proper patient for the first time in my life. Before that day, 13 March 2020, I had not had to sleep overnight in a hospital as a patient – if you excused a voluntary admission for one night in 1988. I had slept in various hospital rooms for close to one-tenth of my professional working life – in doctors' call duty rooms, staff rooms, meetings rooms, side rooms, patients' beds in unoccupied 'side rooms,' and doctors' standard rooms whilst on night duty. Still, in all these circumstances, it had been voluntary, avoidable, but necessary. I had been the doctor who decided, pronounced, arranged, and carried out surgical operations on hapless women. This time however, I was the patient, and this was no ordinary surgery – all four hours of it and five hours altogether under general anaesthesia. I had a cannula inserted into a vein at the back of my left hand at about 9 am.

When I woke up in the recovery room, it was 4:30 pm. I saw the clock, mumbled a "thank you" to the nearest nurse, and lapsed back into sleep. I was under anaesthesia for five hours. My operation lasted for four hours – much longer than was anticipated by the surgeons. The patients who were supposed to follow me on the operation list had their operations canceled because mine had eaten deep into their scheduled time. Unfortunately for these patients, the notorious coronavirus pandemic-induced lockdown of services and public movement in 2020 was announced ten days after my surgery. It would not be eased for another six months during which only *urgent* cases were attended to, and a second wave followed soon after, necessitating further lockdowns. *'Urgent'* in medical parlance refers to life-threatening conditions that can take life in a matter of minutes or hours and therefore require prompt or *emergency* action. Medical conditions under this category include ongoing heavy bleeding, bleeding into the brain, obstruction of blood flow to the bowel, water-logged lungs, heart attacks, acute stroke, and impending rupture of the womb during a woman's labour. Others are premature detachment of the placenta (afterbirth) from the womb in advanced pregnancy, a baby whose head is delivered but its body is stuck in the birth canal (shoulder dystocia), bone fractures, inability to pass urine (retention) and acute poisoning. These are the stuff that an average Accident and Emergency room handles regularly.

In my career as a Gynaecologist who practised during the era before the explosion of keyhole surgery, I performed major surgery on more than five thousand women, most of them being abdominal hysterectomies and Caesarean sections. But none of the 5000 tummies that I cut open prepared me for my own single experience! Never once did I know what each woman felt the next day after surgery. The single night I spent in Blackburn Royal Infirmary in 1988 was a voluntary admission for a minor procedure: my large belly button was surgically tucked in, and I was in and out in a jiffy. My innards were not tampered with, and I was on my feet straight away. I didn't feel what my women felt – until 2020, nearly two years after I had retired from the British National Health Service.

By 7 pm, after that prolonged sleep following my surgery, I was wheeled into my ward, my home, for the following three days. I was groggy. I could only hear nurses coming and going, doing their TPRs.[1] They were checking that I was not bleeding and that my oxygen saturation was not dropping off. I didn't sleep that night because I have had an almighty sleep during the day. I hardly sleep for more than five hours in one single stretch due to years of disruption of my sleep pattern by my professional demands in and around the Labour Ward, so I was not surprised by insomnia. All night long I could hear the struggles and discomfort of the two other men in my cubicle. Both of them were much older than me. The

---

[1] TPR = Temperature, Pulse, and Respiration – observations that nurses make on inpatients to determine progress and detect early warning signs of deterioration. These days, pulse oximetry or oxygen saturation is added to TPR.

gentleman who was directly opposite me has had a tube inserted into his stomach which made coughing up difficult. He coughed and spluttered all through the night and seemed not able to get rid of phlegm. Diagonally across me, his counterpart has had a major abdominal surgery, also for cancer. He was the more stable of the two. Our third ward mate was just to my left. He was younger, perhaps about my agemate. He had his operation a couple of days previously and was going to be discharged the following day.

As the sun rose the day after my surgery, the nurses came to check my tubes, drains, catheter and cannula. I needed to mobilize, change positions (to prevent developing blood clots) and try to cough up the phlegm that had built up inevitably over the previous twenty-four hours. That was when my trouble began. And that was when I recognized the almightiness of God and the distress of postoperative patients.

Prior to coming into the hospital, when my wife, children, and I had been praying, we had usually thanked God for each new morning, for our food, and our safety. However, on this bed, I saw a new dimension to a life of gratitude. Each day of my life, I had jumped out of bed when waking up or, if still tired from a previous night's exertion, slunk off it like it was a right rather than a privilege. The nurse told me she would help me to sit up, and she brought several pillows to support me. She taught me how to alter my posture in bed by using the electronic control, and two of them came to help me sit up. I couldn't because my tummy ached so much. I wanted to cough, but I couldn't because the pain was horrendous. For both sitting or coughing, I needed to use the pair of abdominal muscles called *rectus abdominis* that bend our spines, however as they had been pierced in four places, they were very sore. Don't forget that the surgeons would have been rummaging inside my abdominal cavity for about three or four hours and touching the ultra-sensitive transparent covering of our internal organs called the *peritoneum*.

The nurses understood and were supportive, gently encouraging me inch by painful inch, second by agonizing second. Much later, I asked to get out of bed and sit up in a chair – with their help, of course. My weight, age, and surgery placed me in a high-risk group of people who could develop a blood clot in the leg. If such a clot became detached, it would be swept by blood circulation to the lungs where it could lodge, prevent oxygen exchange, and lead to death.

I needed to sit up: that was not voluntary, did not need my consent, and was their remit. But this was near impossible to do in my state. I was encouraged to wriggle to the edge of the bed where I could sit up and find it easier to get out of bed, but that was easier said than done. I tried to raise my right foot but could not. The pain was lancinating. The nurse helped. I tried to drag the left foot after the right – same difficulty. When I eventually sat at the edge, I could not lever myself out of bed – my spine would not bend. After all, my muscles would not contract because I could not muster the effort required to contract them for the sheer excruciating pain that any attempt engendered. This struggle continued for two more days but the pains gradually decreased. I was well enough to be discharged home four days after surgery, having spent an extra day under observation because I threw up on the day I should have been going home.

About a week after my surgery, when I was already back home, I could bend freely and get off the bed without much difficulty. The difference was very stark. It was then that I thought of how many times in my life that I had got out of bed within five seconds of waking up because I wanted to, without pain or limitation of movement or a nurse's assistance, and how often I had not stopped to thank God for that *"easy and routine"* act. It is easy when you are healthy; it is routine when you have done it over and over and over again, and you don't have to measure each step or think about it. Still, as you are reading this, somebody somewhere in the world has just had their abdominal surgery and cannot move as freely as you do. Now, that is "just getting out of bed!" Can you now imagine how many routine things we do each minute of each day, without thinking about them, without deliberately thinking of which muscle to move first, or how much time it might take us? We do about **eight** things physiologically each day. Each of those – called the characteristics of living things, ^{see #975 p138} – involves a complex array of biochemical, anatomical, and physiological processes. If any of these goes awry or is defective, we become ill and may need to visit a doctor – or an ambulance van dispatched to fetch us. The fact that we can do these things every day is a reason to thank God. The fact that we are alive and escape the hard knocks of life is a reason to praise the Lord.

Here is a short assignment: NOW, please, close your eyes and concentrate for just one moment. Then, think of the things you might want to thank God. Most of us cannot find much more than about ten, maybe thirty, reasons for which to thank God. But here in this little volume, I have enumerated over 1,600 reasons to praise the Lord. There are many more reasons, and no man or collection of humans can find all the reasons for which we are indebted to God for our existence and well-being. This thought probably made Charles Wesley to exclaim:

O for a thousand tongues to sing; My great Redeemer's praise.

Somebody else averred, "If I had a thousand tongues, that would still not be enough to praise the Lord."

In this book, I have given some reasons why we should be grateful to God and some notes to explain why some of these reasons are valid and apt. I have drawn from my medical knowledge of how our body is wonderfully composed. I have outlined, to some extent, the unseen, silent workings of our various body parts and the harmony of the symphony of our body's orchestra, all of which bolstered the Psalmist's assertion that we were wonderfully and fearfully made. We are a marvel. A human body is a piece of ultra-genius work of art and science, a well-oiled multifunctional engine. The basic unit of our body is called the cell. A cell cannot be seen by the naked eye except the largest of them all – a woman's egg from her ovary. Cells collect together to form tissues, like blood, skin, or bone. A drop of blood contains ten trillion red cells. A collection of tissues makes up organs like the heart, kidney, or liver; a group of organs make up systems, such as the digestive or cardiovascular system. All the systems combine to make the human body: digestive, nervous, musculo-skeletal, respiratory, renal, cardiovascular, endocrine, renal and reproductive.

Even some tiny cells in our bodies, like the cardiac cell or the spermatozoon, are beautiful works of art, science, chemistry, and marvel. You have to be a doctor to appreciate the complexities and the thought processes in making each cell and grouping them for specific purposes that interact seamlessly with other groups of cells of different systems that make for a healthy individual. The Lord is great and greatly to be praised!

The chapters deal with the Godhead, the creation of man, man's physical environment, the human body in health, animals and plants.

Let everything that has breath praise the Lord - Psalm 150:6

Chapter 1 | GOD

"Praise ye the Lord. Praise the Lord from the heavens, praise him in the heights." Psalm 148:1

All things praise thee, Lord, Most High.
Heaven and earth and tree and skies,
All were for Thy glory made
That Thy greatness thus displayed,
Should all worship bring to thee;
All things praise thee: Lord, may we.
George William Conder (1821-1874)

Our reasons for praising God include:

1. His Omnipotence – power (Ps 147:5; Jer. 10:12)
2. His Omnipresence – presence (Ps 139: 7-8)
3. His Omniscience – knowledge (Ps 139:2-4)
4. His Love for us (p44)
5. His Majesty
6. His Creation
7. His gift of the Holy Spirit
8. His gift of His Son, Jesus Christ
9. His plan of salvation for a lost world
10. His power and His might
11. All His creation
12. That He created us
13. Formed us out of dust
14. Made us in His image
15. That he made us beautifully
16. That he made us wonderfully (Ps 139:14)

#16 WONDERFULLY MADE – Note 1

I will praise thee; for I am fearfully and wonderfully made: Psalm 139:14

The science of how we are formed in the womb is called Embryology. Imagine some of the many processes that happen simultaneously. Imagine that each human (and animal life) starts from the union of two eggs, one from the mother and the other from the father. These fuse up (fertilization), and straightway the fusion (zygote) starts to divide along. After about a week, we have a flat sheet of identical cells. By the second week, some of these cells group together, and each group starts to develop into different organs that will make up systems. The collection of systems makes up the body. The group that will become the heart, for example, begins to acquire electrical activity, and by the third week, the heart starts to beat rhythmically and will do so until the day of death! The group that will become the stomach begins to acquire the ability to secret and tolerate a concentrated acid – hydrochloric acid – while the group that will become the brain starts to develop the ability to convey nervous impulses. What makes each group turn to different organs is unknown, but **something** does steer them into what they become. Man, as yet, does not know *it*. Some cells become blood, some digestive cells, some bone, others nerve cells or muscle cells. Any disturbance of these processes will lead to a pronounced deformity in the new born baby. Each faculty does not lose its collective ability or get mixed up. The scenario is like a large city council where a managing director divides all the workforce into groups and sends them on their way. Some are the office administrators, some the sanitation department, others the food processors, some, the revenue collectors, some wastes' disposal, another set, the law enforcement and lastly, the protection unit.

As time goes on, each organ modifies itself, multiplies in bulk, undergoes remodelling, jettisons parts that are no more needed, and becomes more refined, or as embryologists say, specialized.

For example, consider the hand: it is a solid tissue to start with, but enzymes dissolve away the flesh that lies between the finger bones such that five distinct fingers later appear in the newborn baby. If those enzymes fail to eat away the flesh to create the clefts between the fingers, the newborn baby will have a clubbed hand with one, two, three, or four fingers – an abnormality. Spare a thought that whilst this is going on, the pattern of lines crisscrossing the hand is emerging, and, it is NOT random. It is so unique to each individual that its uniqueness is used to isolate and identify individuals amongst several millions. It is the basis of fingerprinting which forensic investigators use to identify criminals. Science continues to come up with human traits that are unique and are therefore being used in passport control and in banking. Retinal eye display is now used at immigration controls and "as passwords" in accessing smartphone applications and bank accounts. Blood groups and Human Leucocyte Antigens (HLA) had been used in the past. The latest in this chain is voice recognition technology. Science will probably discover more characteristics unique to each individual in future.

Elsewhere in the body, a man's testicles hang out in a bag called the scrotum. Testicles are actually abdominal organs. They develop inside the abdomen but, by divine grace, move outside the abdominal cavity. Just before a male child is born, each testicle migrates along a tunnel in the groin (inguinal canal) on either side, simultaneously (as if under some supernatural order) and settles in the scrotum where the temperature is about two degrees Celsius cooler than obtains in the core of the body (36.9^0 Celsius). This is the temperature that is optimum, correct and conducive for a man's eggs (spermatozoa) to develop. In the cooler sanctum of the scrotal bag, the eggs will not be subjected to the adverse high body temperature that is inimical to human reproduction. Just two degrees cooler, but it matters. Men whose underwear (briefs, knickers, and Y-fronts) are too tight and whose testicles are pressed too close to the body may have low sperm counts, and in adulthood, their female partners may have infertility. All these were foreseen and sorted out by the Almighty God when He was fashioning us. He made us in ways that made the Psalmist exclaim that we are "***wonderfully made.***"

17. That He made us completely
18. That He made us intelligently
19. That He made us thoughtfully
20. Being intelligent, we can handle tools
21. We can also multitask.
22. He imbued us with wisdom.
23. Has done great things for us (Ps 126)
24. The Earth is full of His goodness (Ps 119:64)
25. He established order in the heights of heaven (Job 25:1)
26. And established order on Earth (Note #2, page 25).

27. ORDERLINESS IN NATURE

There is an ongoing debate between creationists and evolutionists about how man and our universe came into being. For those who believe that man was created, the credit is ascribed to God, the creative force. Wherever we look in nature, we see a great deal of orderliness: the perfect symmetry of flower petals, of flower calyxes, the florets on a sunflower, the concentric rings of an onion, growth rings in trees, grains on a comb of maize corn, the marking patterns on the butterfly, zebra, badger, snakes, and bird of paradise.

Other notable examples include the formation by which migrating birds fly, the seven colours of the rainbow, the perfect hexagonal geometry of the honeycomb, the limbs of a crab or centipede, the planets that orbit the sun, the red blood corpuscle, the bones of the human skeleton, the pairing of our internal organs and the balanced setting of our teeth. Further examples are the regularity of the four seasons in the year, the constant distance between the planets, and the cyclicity of their revolutions around the sun, the rings on the planet Saturn, the arrangement of peas in a pod, the web of a spider, and the spiral pattern of a snail seashell.

In the above examples, where the object is inanimate, like the rainbow and growth rings, the designs are deliberate, reproducible repetitive, and consistent. The rainbow always retains its uniqueness while living organisms pass on their characteristics to their offspring. It is doubtful that a world that evolved out of chaos would arrange itself in an orderly fashion that recurs without outside intelligence. A sun with no intelligence or inbuilt powers is unlikely to organize sequential and perpetual obedience of planets to revolve around it year in, year out. Fishes with scales have the scales overlapping efficiently – even their predators can swallow them quickly because their fins and spikes point backward. A forward-pointing fin or spike will make swallowing impossible, spell the death of predators and the extinction of all species.

28. He breathed the breath of God into our nostrils
29. He gave us life
30. He gave us occupations and jobs to do
31. He gave us supervision
32. He gave us instructions
33. He gave us emotions
34. Imbued us with wisdom and helps us to think
35. He gave us a free choice in life
36. Does not, will not, force any man to worship Him
37. He is constantly dropping signs for us that He loves us
38. Always wants to fellowship with us
39. Always wants us to recognize Him as our Creator-friend
40. He gives us health
41. He is always imbuing our bodies with self-healing capabilities. (note #3, below).

41. HEALING

There was a saying in my undergraduate medical days that "if you had a cold, and you took medications, it would clear up in seven days, but if you took no drugs, it would clear up in a week." In other words, drugs make no difference to the outcome because **the body heals itself.**

But how?

Our bodies are equipped to heal most injuries and diseases. If we had a bacterial infection and took antibiotics, the antibiotics do not heal us – they merely inhibit or kill off the bacteria that are causing the disease and thereby enhance the ability of the body to heal itself. Surgical doctors cut and stitch, but the healing of wounds is a miracle that involves the formation of new cells, collagen and new blood vessels. Man cannot do these; only God does. Ambrose Pare, a 16th century physician to the French King Louis IV, recognising the providential power of God, said of his patient Captain Rat, "I bandaged him, God healed him." (*Je le pansai, Dieu le guerit*). The Latin rendition is "*Natura sanat, medicus curat morbus.*"

Sometimes when we work in the kitchen or a workshop, we mistakenly cut our fingers. Or, in childhood, we suffer a nose bleed. In addition to those times of carelessness, every woman starts to menstruate once a month from about the age of twelve to about fifty. This bleeding from the womb usually stops spontaneously after about five days because of an inbuilt mechanism in every human body. It is called blood coagulation or clotting. And this is how it happens:

Blood that we see is made up of four components. If you put a sample of blood in a test tube and stand it for a few minutes, you will notice it separates into three layers. The bottom half will be red as it contains red blood cells (RBC). Red cells give blood its red colour because they contain an iron-bearing protein, *haemoglobin* which carries oxygen to all tissues and returns "spent air" – *carbon dioxide* – to the lungs where we exhale it.

In the upper half of the test tube will be a straw-coloured liquid layer, plasma. It is the fluid in which all blood cells are suspended. It carried nutrients, mainly glucose, to the tissues. Burning down glucose produces the energy that we need for effort, movement, and so forth.

The interphase between the red cells and the plasma is a thin buff made up of white blood cells (which fight infections) and some brown cells called platelets. Platelets and plasma combine to stop us from haemorrhaging to death when we suffer cuts. First, certain proteins in plasma called *clotting factors* weave a network of webs at the bleeding site. Then platelet cells, which are sticky by nature, get caught up in the nets and gradually grow into lumps that we see as clots as they adhere to one another. In time, the clot acts as a plug that seals up the cut end of the blood vessel. If we dislodge the clot, the process starts again. This process happens after each menstrual period and after childbirth, when the afterbirth has sheared off the interior aspect of our wombs and a large, raw, haemorrhaging surface is created. Without the innate mechanisms of clotting, women will die; man will succumb to death from tiny cuts because, firstly, we have a finite amount of blood in our body, and when we lose about half of it, we are likely to die. Secondly, the amount of clotting factors we have is also limited. In cases where blood loss is heavy and continuing, we exhaust all the clotting factors that we have in reserve, and blood flows out of us interminably.

There is a type of snake venom – haemotoxin – which destroys clotting factors and causes the victim to bleed to death. To confuse issues, viper venom causes the clotting of our blood and the victim of a bite dies because blood coagulates into a jelly and stops flowing, resulting in oxygen starvation of tissues! That is the reason that doctors store **TWO** types of haemotoxin antivenom – one for treating those whose blood fails to clot leading to death by exsanguination (bleeding to death), and another, the opposite – for those whose blood are clotting abnormally, turning blood into a jelly!
Women who die from excessive bleeding during childbirth have usually exhausted the body's store of clotting factors. Experienced doctors usually obtain clotting factors from *blood banks* to be infused into such women to save lives. However, a smaller percentage of heavy bleeding results from traumatic tear to certain tissues: rupture of the uterus, laceration of the cervix, and tears of the vagina and perineum.

For these acts of God, the in-built mechanism to arrest small bleeds, the ability of a woman's body to control blood loss from the womb without her being aware of the biochemical processes, we ought to praise the Lord. Women who menstruate normally, or give birth easily, ought always to praise the Lord.

42. He heals our diseases (Ps 103:3)
43. Teaches our hands to prosper (Deut 18:18; 30:9)
44. Adds blessings to the labour of our hands
45. Perfects that which concerns us (Ps 138:8)
46. He knows them that trust Him (Nahum 1:7)
47. Upholds those who fall (Ps 145:14)
48. Reassures us and tells us not to be afraid (Is 41:10)
49. Taught us to rest after our labours (Ex 20:10)
50. He lifts us up (Ezek 43:5)
51. Pardons our sins (Ps 103:3)
52. He does not mark our transgressions – otherwise, no one will stand (Ps 130:3)
53. He revives us (Ps 138:7)
54. He protects us (Ps 121:5)

54   THE PROTECTION OF GOD – 1
(Unlocked car doors)

We have to thank God daily for our protection. We take numerous measures to ensure that we do not leave ourselves needlessly exposed to danger. We lock our gates, front doors, take out accident insurances and home insurances. We install smoke alarm systems, protect our computers from being hacked, use coded passwords to protect our bank accounts, lock car doors, install car alarms and immobilizers and many other preventive and protective features. All these are commendable, but ultimately, safety is of God.

Some of us might be able to recall instances in our lives when we absent-mindedly forgot to lock doors, turn off water taps, switch off cooking stoves, or perhaps, left our car keys conspicuously on the door or in the ignition! When we narrowly escape disasters, we thank God; however, most days, when things go smoothly, we must thank God, too.

I travelled to Birmingham one summer day in 2017 in the company of a friend who was on holiday from Lesotho, where he was a professor of genetics. We had arranged to meet with a surgeon friend to try to investigate the untimely death of a mutual friend (and his wife) in a house fire in an Eastern European country because we suspected he had no close relatives in the United Kingdom. We parked my car about two streets away from the hospital where the deceased wife's secretary worked. We probably left in a hurry because when we returned about an hour later, I was shocked at the sight that confronted me: I had left the boot and one rear door wide open. The window on my side – the driver's side – was wound down. My wallet was in the car, and we had left valuables on the back seat. I would not know how many people passed that way in one hour behind Birmingham's second largest hospital, but God, in His mercy, did not allow any of them to be tempted to tamper with my car nor take anything that I had carelessly left in full public glare.

If that did not tell me that it is God, not my carefulness, that helps and protects me, then the next episode, about 18 months after that episode, was even worse.

I had just returned from holidays and needed a visit to my doctor at his surgery. For some strange reason, I took both sets of my car keys along. I parked the car near the kerb along the highway to Liverpool but directly in front of the surgery. I went in to see the doctor, had my consultation, and was back to the car within fifteen minutes. As I approached my car, I pressed the remote control to unlock the car doors, but I did not hear the usual clicking sound. The lock was not on, so I took my seat, ready to start the ignition. At that moment, I realized that the engine was running anyway and what I had in hand was the spare key! In other words, for fifteen minutes after disembarking from the car, I had left the car with the engine running by the roadside and disappeared into the building. Any of many things could have happened, such as a curious joyrider driving the car away effortlessly. It was completely my fault but God in His mercy covered my nakedness and forgave my carelessness. I thought to myself that I had forfeited the car that day, and each day that I possessed it thereafter was a bonus from God. One reason, therefore, that I will always praise the Lord is His gracious keeping and preservation of whatever He allows me to possess.

THE PROTECTION OF GOD – 2 (Night Flights)

If you have taken an overnight flight from one of the world's capital cities to another country, you must have marvelled at the activities at the airports. I arrived at John F Kennedy airport in June 2019 to join a waiting queue of hundreds of people and many busy airport officials. At another time in Lagos, Nigeria, while waiting to check in for a London-bound flight via Paris, my Air France flight was cancelled because there had been a workers' strike at *Charles de Gaulle* airport in Paris. All passengers booked on that flight were being firmed out to alternative airplanes – some to Lufthansa, others to KLM, Turkish Airlines, and so on. I was fortunate to be put aboard a British Airways flight to London. The airport was a beehive of activity. Our flight was not until just before midnight, and I watched several planes depart.

As we landed at Heathrow, we queued up for the usual border immigration clearances just as at the JFK. The usual phenomenon of several groups of people arriving periodically in batches and joining us swelled the throng in the queues. Each passenger and each plane had travelled through the night from countries such as India, Ghana, South Africa, Singapore, Brazil and the USA. At any given time in the previous night's sky, several planes were in the air, each under the staff of *Ground Control* of whichever country's airspace they were traversing.

In the USA, for instance, I saw a visual picture of the airplanes in the sky at a particular time. It was mind-boggling and even more remarkable that, adding private jets and helicopters to these fleet, mid-air collisions were not as common as people tripping over in the street! Air accidents are relatively rare, and because they seldom take place, it is easy to assume that we have the prerogative to travel safely, freely, and unhindered at all times. The opposite is the truth – that each flight is a challenge for the crew, the plane, and the officials who give permissions to take off, land or stack planes over busy airports. Sometimes, the niceties give way to emergency landings for planes in distress.

I know, as a doctor, that medical accidents are usually likened to aeronautical industry mishaps in that doctors are constantly being trained, advised and guided to prevent disasters rather than wait for accidents to happen before they learn harsh lessons. Airline companies know that any accidents will result in significant loss of lives. Each plane is therefore regularly serviced and rendered in good working order. Similarly, but less expansively, a doctor must hone his or her skills before laying hands on humans on an operating table. Several years go into making a surgeon. And, regardless of the number of times a doctor has carried out a particular procedure, he or she must approach each operation with utmost care and respect.

During my career as an Obstetrician and Gynaecologist, I cut open thousands of women's abdomens – mostly for hysterectomies and Caesarean Sections. The fact that I had performed many of these procedures previously was never a license to be sloppy or overconfident with the next. There was even an aphorism that the operation that a surgeon underestimates as "an easy job" tends to turn out to be a nightmare. Each doctor would want their patient to be very slim, fit, and healthy and having surgery for the first time. If they have had a previous surgical operation, tissues tend to be stuck to each other (*adhesions*) and the separation of tissues along the natural planes of the body will be and challenging. Any undue haste or inattention to detail might damage tissues or cause heavier bleeding than necessary. Patients that are overweight have thicker abdominal walls due to excess body fat. The doctor has to carefully cut through these to arrive at the site where the real problem lies.

From experience, sometimes, a surgeon might need an additional doctor to physically retract a thick-walled abdominal cut that is threatening to collapse onto the operating field and limit visualization. In slimmer patients, employing some instruments (*retractors*) to keep the cut surfaces apart usually suffices. For all these, I would need to maintain extra vigilance and be conscious of the fact that each operation was a challenge, a test of mental mettle and skill, and that the human body, as the patient, must be treated with the greatest respect. Whenever a patient emerges from an operating room safely, their doctors and operating theatre staff would have gone through these processes, and the patient needs to thank God. And the surgeon as well!

Likewise, each time we disembark from an airplane, we have many reasons for which to be grateful to God. We also have the pilots to thank, the cabin crew to commend for the assistance, instructions, and perhaps refreshments they give. We need to thank the ground staff as well, because they ensure orderly checking in and clearance of our credentials to board our flights or permission to enter our desired foreign ports. Besides, we can thank God for stabilizing our planes amid air turbulence, preventing mid-air collisions, allowing the landing gears to deploy safely, not allowing engine or instrumental failure, birds to be sucked into engines, and many more.

Upon landing, we expect our luggage to appear on the carousel. Still, we seldom think of the intricacy and agility of the luggage handlers to accurately label our bags, send them on the right flights, get onto the correct connecting flights and reach the appropriate terminals at the relevant airports. Often, we simply pick up our luggage and exit the airport, but we make complaints if our luggage was lost. But where is the *'Thank You'* when things go right?

THE PROTECTION OF GOD – 3 (Freak Accidents-1)

We take precautions daily to prevent accidents and disasters: helmet for bicycle riders, shoes to avoid stubbing our toes, reasonably low vehicle speeds to prevent road traffic accidents, rear fog lights to avoid being rammed from behind, not talking whilst eating to avoid choking, regularly servicing of our cars to avoid an inconvenient break down in awkward, unsafe areas, hand washing to prevent germs and infections, and so forth. These are sensible things we must do. However, there are instances when circumstances are beyond human control.

We might be able to recollect some air crashes when planes went down in residential areas. People who were safely cocooned in their homes could be killed or burnt to death by such unfortunate mishaps.

In a particular plane accident in Northern Nigeria in January 1973, an aircraft crashed just short of the runway due to landing gear collapse and bad weather. The irony was that 26 passengers survived out of 193, whereas amongst the dead were eight people on the ground who were never on the plane!

Somebody said of the precautions that we take, *"Safety is not the absence of danger but the presence of God."* When we witness events like this airplane accident, landslides, mudslides that wipe out houses, and flash floods that sweep away human dwellings, we acknowledge that some people are unfortunate. Our hearts should go out to them. For those who escape, by design or fortuity, we have cause to praise the Lord.

THE PROTECTION OF GOD – 4 (Framed Up)

A Yoruba twilight tale from Nigeria was of a monkey punished for a matter she knew nothing about. The tortoise, the archetypal and ubiquitous hero of Yoruba twilight tales, wanted to exact revenge for the monkey's insolence. The tortoise prayed, *"Deliver us from evil, especially from matters that we know nothing about,"* but the monkey had refused to acknowledge this with an "Amen."

The tortoise went about his plot by marinading large pieces of meat that he delicately cooked to a very delectable taste. He made sure he ate it at Tiger's house. The tiger caught the aroma and begged for some. The tortoise volunteered only the last piece to the tiger. Tiger ate it and wanted more. The Tortoise explained that she had given away all that she brought from the supplier. The tiger became hungry and impatient for more. He asked the tortoise what he had been given to eat and why it tasted so divine. "It is the monkey's excrement," Tortoise replied. The tiger went in search of the monkey to have some of his faeces. When the monkey moved her bowel, the smell was redolent and the taste awful, quite unlike the tortoise's morsel. "Please, produce the sweet variety," pleaded the tiger. The monkey obliged, but it was just as foul. Feeling mocked and disrespected, the tiger held the monkey up by its two forelimbs and slapped the monkey on her tummy. "The sweet one," he demanded again and again. The more the monkey emptied its bowel contents, the more beating she got from the tiger because the smell remained odious. Her ordeal was over only after Tiger was exhausted and let go. The tortoise, hiding out of view, was satisfied and melted away.

In real life, some people go out looking for somebody – anybody – on whom to inflict pain. Some people plan a "crash for cash" accident and will deliberately crash into *any* car; there are girls who have stayed out beyond the time permitted by their parents and so want somebody to blame. They could cook up stories of physical assault, attempted rape, or full-on sexual assault instead of owning up to their parents that they had been careless. There have been disturbed people who opened fire on innocent bystanders or school children, and there are terrorists who plant explosive devices in public places. In some cases, pedestrians emerge out of nowhere and throw themselves at a passing car. In each of these cases, the perpetrator wants a victim but who that victim would be is indiscriminate and random. That is why the tortoise's prayer is relevant. The Lord's prayer might have inspired it in Matthew 6:13, "*And lead us not into temptation, but deliver us from evil.*"

Every day, we need to be delivered from evil. We need to escape from snipers, dangerous people, deranged people, and dangers that lurk in the dark, waiting for just anybody to pass by to be trapped. As long as we do not fall victim to these sorts of attacks, we have reasons to thank God.

THE PROTECTION OF GOD – 5 (Marriage)

If we have a spouse, we probably have gone through meeting with a boy or girl we love. Courtship follows, then marriage and the setting up of a home and a family – not necessarily in that particular order. What can be more straightforward? What can go wrong?
Plenty! If your path to marriage was as smooth as stated above, then thank God again for your life path. And you may thank God every day for the same.

A 20 year-old Australian man met a beautiful girl of the same age. They fell in love and decided to get married. They got a mortgage and started building a house. Then, everything turned sour. The police arrested the man and took him in for interrogation. He did not know his offense and felt like he was watching a fictional movie. They read the charges to him: repetitive domestic violence and rape of his fiancée. After overcoming his shock, he categorically denied that anything of the sort ever took place. He was remanded in Goulburn, Australia's maximum security prison, for four months while his parents genuinely feared that he would die in detention at the hands of its brutal inmates. A woman police officer started to handle the case and stated that she believed the man was guilty. However, the more she delved into it, the more convinced she became about allegations that did not match the facts and findings. From interviewing the complainant, she discovered that she had been lying all along. The man was released while the woman was found guilty and sentenced. The ramifications of the whole case were yet to be concluded at the time of writing this book. The man's parents explained that their legal bill, as of September 2020, was more than three hundred and fifty thousand Australian dollars ($350,000), having remortgaged their house and incurred huge debts. The six years of legal tussle had a damaging effect on their marriage. All these stemmed from two lovers' chance meeting.

The lesson here is that an average couple finds love, gets engaged and gets married. Compared to the narrative above, such couples have it easy, not by sagacity or prudence, but by the grace of God. Whatever we do in life that does not have complications or adversely affect our kith and kin must draw God's praise from our lips and within our hearts.

THE PROTECTION OF GOD – 6 (Freak Accidents-2)

Most of us have often seen accidents that were, at best unfortunate for the victims. Sometimes, a girl walking along a street suddenly disappears into a maintenance hole; the ground literarily opens up and swallows a few houses because of previous mining activities or fantastic underground river erosions; a tsunami, an earthquake, or a volcano that is throwing a blanket of poisonous miasma over a village. The Yoruba people of Nigeria have a prayer which roughly translates as *"Dear God, do not let me travel on the day that the Road is hungry for human meals."*

Mr. Roberto Carlos Fernandez, a 51year-old Brazilian in Ipatinga, was walking legally against traffic on the pedestrian pavement in February 2020, alongside his wife. The dual carriageway had a large central reservation of about fifty meters beautifully planted with grass and trees – the sort that kids play ball games on. A security camera captured a loose tyre from a vehicle on the other side of the road hurtling in at great speed and arrowed in like a heat-seeking missile, bounced up, and hit Roberto plum on the back of his head (occiput). He was knocked out, and his face was squashed as he hit the ground. His wife, oblivious of the preceding events, suddenly found that he was out cold. Passers-by rushed to his aid and took him to hospital. Thankfully, reports said that he survived and recovered after having had fractured skulls and ribs. His was a classic case of being in the wrong place at the right time, *Arinsesesi,* or walking into trouble.

Every day when we walk down the street, jog, run, ride a bicycle, play in the open field or take a stroll in the woods, we are liable to such freak accidents: it is the mercy of God that keeps us safe.

55. Hedges us behind and before (Ps 139)
56. Bears us on eagles' wings (Exodus 19:4)
57. Provides for us
58. Feeds us
59. Provides food for us in due season (Psalm 145:15)
60. Allows us to have a choice of menu
61. And the benefit of eating cooked, warm or hot meals* (see Story 47, p144)
62. He redeems us
63. Daily loads us with benefits
64. He wakes us up each morning (it's not the alarm!)

64. WAKING UP IN THE MORNING. Note #10, p39

EACH NIGHT when we go to bed, we are oblivious of our surroundings from the moment we drift into a deep sleep. Many dangers pass at night. Our brains rest, as does our body. Deep sleep is like being under general anaesthesia. To come back to *'the land of the living'* is a miracle. One author wrote, *"if you think it was your alarm that woke you up this morning, try putting an alarm clock beside a corpse."* No matter how loud an alarm clock may sound, it is true that it cannot and will never wake a dead man. We must thank God every day that we rise to see the light of a new day.

World Health statistics state that 56 million people die worldwide every year. That comes down to nearly 1.8 people dying every second, or 6,392 per hour. Therefore, each night, in the seven hours of sleep from going to bed at 11 pm to rising at 6am, (7x6392) or 44,744 people have passed away by the time we wake up. Each day, therefore, that we are not numbered amongst that number, we ought to be thanking God.

58 GOD GIVES US OUR FOOD IN SEASON (Alive!) 11

The eyes of all look to you, and you give them their **food** *at the proper time. Ps 145:15*

Have you ever had food when you wanted it? Have you ever had to choose what you would eat from a set of menu? Did you eat any warm food yesterday? Have you eaten at least three different types of food in the past seven days? If you have answered "Yes" to any or most of those questions, then you might have reasons to praise the Lord.

A 15-man amateur Rugby team took off on a chartered plane from Montevideo in Uruguay for a match in Chile on another side of the Andes in October 1972. Five crew members, 25 friends, and family, including five women, joined them aboard the military plane. The trip was expected to last for five days. The weather was terrible and forced an overnight stay in Mendoza, Argentina, at the foothills of the Andes, by the Chilean border. The next day, *Friday 13* October, the plane took off to conclude its journey. Poor visibility, strong winds, and foul weather caused the plane to crash into a snow-filled ravine high up in the Andes. Rescue efforts did not locate them in the vast expanse of snowfields. Sighting was made difficult because the plane's roof was painted white. There were instant deaths and varying degrees of injuries, but some escaped without significant trauma. They could not make radio contact with rescue teams, and hope gradually faded after a few days. The plane's tail broke off with the original impact, but the fuselage was intact and provided shelter from the elements.

Realising that they had been given up for dead, they began to ration the little food available. When food was exhausted, even the toothpaste that was among the luggage had to be apportioned. The little water available was what could be obtained by melting snow when the sun was shining. There was a lot of improvisation, and they had to contend with at least one deadly avalanche that took out two of them. Eventually, they completely ran out of food – any food.

At this stage, they were at the point of starving to death and two of them did an unthinkable thing to keep them alive: they took tiny slices off one of the corpses that the icy conditions have preserved well. Gradually, all survivors joined in and partook in this survival fare, but this also ran out after several weeks. Only then did they realize that to stay up in the rarified environment with no prospect of sustenance or rescue, they were merely delaying the inevitable. Their only option was to find a way to come down the mountain to make contact with civilization. At that stage, the 16 who were still surviving contributed warm clothing and food for two volunteers. They sent the duo away amidst tears that if they failed, they would all be doomed. The two gallant members would have to brave treacherous terrains, neck-deep snow, steep rock faces, and several miles to seek help. They had no compass or navigational tool. After ten days of the arduous trek, they arrived at ground level and soon found villagers who were kind to usher them to the safety of a hut where they told tales of their incredible survival and their friends still trapped high up on the mountains. Within two days, all the 16 survivors had been rescued. It had been 70 days since their plane crashed. Newspapers carried their story with the headline "ALIVE."[2] That became the title of the book and the film that documented their story.

Of all the talking points in this story, perhaps the most touching and didactic is the thought that if we were sufficiently pushed to the wall, we would do things we would not contemplate doing under normal circumstances. We would eat food that we would typically disdain. The plane survivors had no food, had no choice of menu, had no warm food or hot drink, and had to eat whatever was in their vicinity, at freezing temperatures – as long as it was edible.

For these reasons, if we have food and a choice of it, we ought always to praise the Lord.

65. God helps us get up or sit up when we wake (postoperative patients appreciate this more than most of us) *I have alluded to this extensively in the preface. Please see chapter 4 for more

[2] Piers Paul Read: ALIVE!. Arrow Books 2012, London ISBN 9780099574521

physiological processes that go on in our bodies without much thought.

66. Helps us get off the bed each morning (It is one thing to wake up, another to get up, and quite another to get out of bed).

67. Helps us keep our balance straight out of bed.

66 KEEPING OUR BALANCE (Story #12)

One autumn morning in 2018, my wife woke me up from sleep because she had an important message to pass to me. As I woke up and turned to face her, I felt like I was going to fall out of bed, and the room seemed to be spinning, so I quickly reverted to the position that I was in previously – lying on my left side. In a matter of three minutes, everything reverted to normal. It happened a few weeks later, and I conferred with my daughter, a General Practitioner (GP). She not only explained the phenomenon of Benign Paroxysmal Positional Vertigo (BPPV) but suggested I mention it to my doctor. My GP referred me to an Otorhinolaryngologist (a specialist Ear, Nose and Throat surgeon). BPPV occurs when changes in the position of the head such tipping the head backward, lead to sudden vertigo (a feeling that the room is spinning). The scientific basis is this...

Normally, in our inner ear, there are three tiny tubes, *semicircular canals,* whose primary job is to regulate our balance by sensing the position of our head. The canals are lined by tiny sensory hair cells and filled with a fluid, endolymph or *Scarpa fluid.* When our head moves around, the liquid inside them sloshes around and moves the tiny hair cells. These relay messages to our brain of what position we adopt (erect, horizontal, or spiral). The brain is thus able to help us maintain our balance and equilibrium. As we age, chemicals in the fluid crystalise out as calcium carbonate (*otoconia*). Sometimes, these crystals break off the surface linings and brush against the hair processes. That contact is also relayed to the brain which might misinterpret it as meaning we were moving whereas we were still or lying down. The brain, in trying to correct our positions, sends the incorrect information to our eyes. It creates the impression that we are spinning or about to fall out of bed.

The other body systems that help us maintain our balance include our skeleton, muscles, brain (the cerebellum), our ears (the vestibule and semi-circular canals), and our eyes. To appreciate the importance of our eyes in helping us keep our balance, let's conduct a small experiment: Please, stand in a safe place, away from furniture or objects. Put your feet together; then, close your eyes. Within a few minutes, you would be wobbling and losing your balance and feel like keeling over. It does not happen if your eyes were open. On a typical day, we hardly think of all these organs when we stand in a supermarket queue or watch sports from the spectators' stands. This is another reason that should make us thank God for such body processes that make us who we are.

68. Made us two by two, each gender complementing the other
69. Made each mate precisely complementary to the opposite sex
70. Blessed us to reproduce, increase and replenish the Earth
    (Genesis 1:28)
71. Guides us because we are *pilgrims through this barren land*
72. Leads us by still waters (Ps 23:2)
73. Plants us by rivers of pleasure (Jer. 17:8)
74. Anoints our head with oil
75. Made the heaven and the earth (Ps 146:6; Genesis 1:1))

76. Keeps truth forever (Ps 146:6)
77. Executes justice for the oppressed (*ibid*, v7)
78. Gives food to the hungry (Ps 107:9)
79. Satisfies the thirsty (Ps 107: 9)
80. Gives freedom to prisoners (Ps 146:7)
81. Opens the eyes of the blind (v8)
82. Raises those who are bowed down - by disease, affliction, oppression, persecution (Ps 145:14)
83. Loves the righteous (Ps 146:8)
84. Watches over strangers (v9)
85. Shall reign forever (v10)
86. His mercy endures forever (Ps 118:3; Ps 136: 1-36)
87. He turns the rejected stone to the cornerstone (Ps 118:22)
88. Heals our infirmities and blemishes (Exodus 15:26)
89. The Lord is on our side (Ps 124)
90. Watches our coming in and going out (Ps 121)
91. Watches over us (Gen 28:15)
92. Guides our footsteps (Prov 20:24)
93. Prevents us from being swallowed by the flood of life (Ps 124)
94. We shall not die but declare His works (Ps 118:17)
95. Makes the barren woman to have children (Ps 113:9)
96. Makes all things work for our good (Romans 8:28)
97. Turns bad situations around for our good (Gen45:4-8)
98. No matter how bad a situation is, He leaves us some reasons still to be thankful.

97 PRAISING GOD FOR THE BAD TIMES –
The Legend of The Desert Wayfarer.

Should we praise the Lord when things seemingly go wrong or actually go wrong? Sometimes we ask, "Why do the Righteous Suffer?" We frequently hear from experts on Bible matters that "All things work for good to those who love God, and to those who are 'the called' according to His purpose." (Romans 8:28).

A story was told that must challenge us to consider this verse thoroughly.

An adventurer took a trip into the Sahara Desert but soon got hopelessly lost amidst the dunes and unmarked terrain. Having long exhausted his water supply, he came close to dying from thirst, dehydration and exhaustion. At the point when his life was about to expire, he spotted an oasis and used all his remaining energy and willpower to limp to the fertile spot. He knocked on the door of a large hut, and a beautiful lady in her fifties welcomed him with a smile and a knowing pity on her face. He probably had no energy to ask, but the woman understood his greatest and pressing need. She went inside and soon emerged with a bowl of cool crystal-clear water. When she was about to hand the bowl over to the man, she bent down, scooped a handful of sand and dropped it into the water. The man looked at the woman contemptuously but was in no physical shape to refuse the drink. He took a few sips but had to stop to blow the dirt backward before continuing to drink. He continued the stop-start sips until he eventually emptied the bowl except for the sand sediments and debris. He managed a grudging *"Thank you"* as he turned to go away. Away from earshot, he cursed under his breath, being full of anger and disbelief at a wicked woman who took advantage of a man's desperate need and, in doing so, spoilt an excellent act by sheer sadism.

Three years later, the man was passing that way again. This time, he hired two camels and a local guide and packed enough water skins so he wasn't caught out again. He made sure he looked out for the woman and had a burning question for his desert angel-tormentor. He was glad that the woman was still living in the hut. After a cursory exchange of pleasantries, he challenged the woman why she decided three years earlier to soil the water she served him when she knew that his vulnerability and desperation made it irresistible to refuse any water he was offered. Did she not think she was sadistic?

"My dear Sir," the woman explained, "I have lived here long enough and seen many a wayfarer died whilst drinking water to quench their thirst after long wanderings in the hostile, scorching and hot desert sun. I added some dirt to your water because it would slow you down as you sipped it. Many people who came before you drank too rapidly and swallowed a lot of air that choked them. That dirt that angered you so much was deliberately added to prevent you from dying."

The man was speechless and somewhat ashamed when his folly and uninformed misconception were exposed. He realized that he ought to be thanking the woman for her hospitality in offering water and her thoughtfulness to prevent a disaster. Not only was he a conspiracy theorist but a hasty, poor judge. His benefactor was benevolent, but it all appeared to him that she was deliberately cruel.

In the same way, Reader, we sometimes have instances in our lives when it appears that God has thrown sand into our clear water. Instead of expressing gratitude to the God who does well at all times, we moan and murmur at what we think we deserve.

Sometimes we focus on what we want instead of thanking God for what we already have. A man who complains that his job is too arduous may be surprised to find that many men will gladly take his place because they have no job at all. When we desire to own a car, we must stop to think of the man who has only a pushbike. Even the latter must thank God because there are men who go about on their "*footwagons*" (bare feet) and there are those who have no feet at all:

Mr. Babatunde Kewejo, a 39 year-old cab driver in Ibadan, Nigeria was interviewed by *BBC News Pidgin* in 2022. He had no legs! His feet were amputated due to childhood infections but he went on to graduate at university and when governmental employment did not materialise, he plunged into the motor business. He did not allow his disability to be a hindrance to life or to happiness.*

*'Man With No Legs Drives Taxi At Ibadan' BBC News Pidgin (https://www.bbc.com/pidgin/tori-60733083.amp). Accessed 2022

This thought brings us to appreciate Johnson Oatman's hymn, '*Count your Blessings*' ...

"When upon life billows you are tempest-tossed,
When you are discouraged, thinking all is lost,
Count your many blessings name them one by one,
And it will surprise you what the Lord has done." J. Oatman, 1897

99. His tender mercies are over all His works
100. His mercies endure forever. (Ps 118:)
101. His kingdom is everlasting
102. His dominion endures throughout all generations
103. His truth endures forever (Ps 117)
104. Upholds all who fall
105. Raises those who are bowed down
106. Maintains justice for the poor (Ps 140:12)
107. He delights in loving kindness, judgment, and righteousness (Jer. 9:24)
108. He gives all creatures food in due season.
109. Satisfies the desire of every living thing
110. Righteous in ALL His ways. (Ps145:17)

111. Near to all who call upon Him (especially to all who call upon Him in truth)
112. Preserves all who love Him
113. Will destroy **all** the wicked. (Ps 145:20)
114. Cuts into pieces the cords of the wicked (Ps 129:4)
115. He has broken the gates of brass Ps 107:16)
116. And has cut the bars of iron asunder (Ps 107:16)
117. He heals the broken-hearted (Ps 147:3)
118. He binds up their wounds. (Ps 147:3)
119. He counts the numbers of the stars, and He calls them ALL by name (Ps 147:4)
120. God's understanding is infinite (v5)
121. Lifts the humble (Psalm 147:6)
122. Casts the wicked down to the ground (v6)
123. Covers the heavens with clouds (v)8
124. Prepares rain for the Earth. (v8)
125. He makes grass grow on the mountains (8)
126. Gives food to the beasts and birds (v147:9)
127. He does not delight in human strength (v10)
128. Takes pleasure in those who fear Him (v11)
129. Has blessed our children (v13)
130. Makes peace in our borders (v14)
131. Fills us with the finest of the wheat (v14)
132. Teaches our mouths to sing
133. He gives us reasons to sing and praise Him
134. He causes snow to fall, causing cold
135. Then, He sends warmth and melts the snow (v18)
136. His name alone is exalted (Ps 148)
137. He is the I am that I am (Exodus 3:14)
138. The Father of lights (James 1:17)
139. Is a Stronghold in the day of trouble (Nahum 1:7)
140. Is our Shepherd (Ps 23:1)
141. Is our Rock (Ps 144:2)
142. Is our Bulwark (Ps 18:2 - *Young's Literal Translation*)
143. Is our Shield (Ps 144:2)
144. He is our Fortress. (2 Sam 22:3; Psalm 18:2, 31;3. 71:3, 91:2, 144:2)

145. Our Deliverer (ibid; Ps 144:2)
146. Our God (Exodus 20:2)
147. Our Refuge (144:2)
148. Our salvation (Ps 118: 14)
149. Our Strength (Ps 118: 14)
150. Buckler – defender (2 Sam 22:31)
151. The Horn of my salvation (2 Sam 22:3)
152. Our High tower Psalm 18:2. 144:2)
153. The Lifter-up of our heads
154. Is our portion in the land of the living (Ps 142:5)

Stuart K. Hine penned the lyrics of *"How Great Thou Art"* to include this:

O Lord my God! when I in awesome wonder
Consider all the works Thy hand hath made
I see the stars; I hear the mighty thunder
Thy power throughout the universe displayed.

When through the woods and forest glades, I wander
And hear the birds sing sweetly in the trees
When I look down from lofty mountain grandeur
And hear the brook, and feel the gentle breeze

And when I think that God His Son not sparing
Sent Him to die – I scarce can take it in
That on the cross my burden gladly bearing
He bled and died to take away my sin

Then sings my soul, my Saviour God, to Thee
How great Thou art! How great Thou art!
Then sings my soul, my Saviour God, to Thee.
How great Thou art! How great Thou art!

Stuart K. Hine - 1953

155. For His dealings with the patriarchs and our ancestors
156. For delivering His people Israel by a mighty outstretched hand (Deut. 26:8)
157. For the miracles in Egypt
158. For the miracles in the wilderness
159. For daily loading us with benefits
160. For the beauty of His holiness
161. For the holiness of His beauty
162. For the majesty of His presence
163. For the presence of His majesty
164. For the purity of His righteousness
165. For the righteousness of His purity
166. For His divine awe
167. And for the wonder of His divinity
168. For giving us the Law and the Commandments
169. For giving us the Bible
170. For helping the ancients to preserve the Biblical texts for us.

170 THE DEAD SEA SCROLLS Note *14*

*Sometimes, we want to see evidence before we believe, but the way the Lord operates is that we believe **before** we see.* That shows implicit trust in Him, in His power and ability to do far more exceedingly than we can imagine. While some people still doubt the authenticity and origins of the Bible, God, in His mercy, helped humanity to underline an ancient fact in 1947.

The new state of Israel was created by the United Nations in 1948, shortly after the end of the Second World War.

In 1947, a farmer in Qumran, about one mile from the Dead Sea, lost one of his goats. He felt it had fallen into one of the deep ravines amongst the mountains. It was dark down there, and he could not see the bottom of the pit. He therefore threw down a pebble, hoping that it would hit the goat or create a fright that would make it bleat. He was surprised that the sound that echoed back suggested the pebble had hit a hollow object. Curious, he went down to explore. To his amazement, he found a pot that contained a piece of leather with inscriptions on it. He sold it to a cobbler in Damascus. Rather than turn the leather into a pair of shoes, the shoemaker noted that there were some ancient inscriptions on the leather. He sought help to decipher his finding: it was a portion of the Old Testament of the Bible. The people who got the parchment explored the site and found many more pots, each containing different portions of the Bible. They had been well-preserved since some people deposited them there in the first century, about 70 AD, just before or about the time of the Jewish War[3]. More parchments and manuscripts were discovered in 11 caves in 1956. Scientific experts have dated some of the parchments to 330 BC. When my wife and I went to Jerusalem with a group of Christians in 2006, we were glad to visit the *Museum of The Book* (Shrine of the Book) - a museum in Jerusalem that now houses all the pots and parchments collected at the site about 15,000 fragments. The only book of the Bible that was recovered in its entirety was the book of the prophet Jeremiah: other books had bits and pieces missing at the edges.

HOW DID THE BOOKS GET THERE?

About the time of Jesus Christ's ministry, there were four religious sects in Jerusalem: the Pharisees, the Sadducees, the Essenes and the Zealots. The Sadducees were wealthy upper class, who did not believe in the

---

[3] The Jewish War – 75AD. Also known as The Judean War; The Wars of the Jews. It was a war between the Romans and the Jews.

supernatural such as angels, demons, heaven, hell, resurrection, after-life, and eternal punishment. They were more Temple oriented and sided with the Roman rulers.

The Pharisees were closer to the common man, loved the synagogues and believed in oral tradition and emphasized personal piety.

The Essenes were an ascetic sect that practised voluntary poverty, immersion and separation. Persecution by the Roman occupation was severe for believers, and the Essenes moved out into the wilderness in the mountains. The Roman army went after them and barricaded them. The cult did not surrender but hid portions of their scriptures in earthen pots in the crevices.

Discovering these, and seeing that they matched what the world knew as the Bible gave a fillip to believers of our day that God's word had been preserved through the ages. The Zealots opposed Roman rule.

We praise God for this fortune, in particular,

171. That the Essenes preserved the scrolls;
172. That the scripts were well-preserved for our generation
173. That the weather condition of the atmosphere was dry, the humidity around the Dead Sea was low, therefore, conducive to prolonged storage of leather. Had the area been moist, those parchments could have been destroyed by mold or decay!
174. That a goat was lost;
175. That the farmer who lost the goat chose an ingenious way to search for it;
176. That the pebble he threw into the gorge serendipitously hit one of several pots: it could have missed and we would have no Dead Sea Scroll today;
177. That the farmer did not destroy the parchment but sold it on;
178. That the cobbler did not destroy the leather or covert it to a footwear
179. That the people he sold it to successfully translated the ancient writings
180. That a delegation went back to look for more scrolls
181. That they looked in the right places and found more scrolls.

182. For the wisdom and knowledge to translate the Aramaic and Hebrew Bible to Greek
183. For men and women who translated these into all modern languages
184. For the works of translators like Jerome (Latin), William Tyndale (English), and Martin Luther (Greek)
185. For the work of Guttenberg and those who printed the early copies
186. For those who distribute and fund distribution of the Bible
187. For those who teach and explain Scripture.
188. For the richness of Scripture, its stories, literature, lessons and blessings
189. For the ability to own personal copies
190. For the freedom to read Scripture
191. For teaching us the history of God's dealing with the patriarchs
192. For the relevance of Scripture to our lives
193. For the salvation message that Scripture brings
194. For revealing to the laity the full gospel message and truth
195. For the prophets and the saints gone before us as examples of faith
196. For the promise of God's blessings
197. For giving us His holy angels to guide us
198. For giving us advisers, counsellors and mentors
199. And the ability to maintain self-control
200. For the blessing that comes from being able to achieve self-control

199 SELF CONTROL IS A CHOICE 15th

As a boy of ten, I was with my father one evening after supper. Something had upset my mother, and for the first and only time in my life, I heard her speak rather impolitely to my dad for a few moments. To every uncomplimentary statement that would have incensed an average man, my father replied, "I thank God."

Even I, a young boy, expected Papa to flip under the barrage, but he never once showed irritation or anger. I was intrigued. Not many days later, my dad and I were on his farm, and as was my custom, I had the chance to ask him questions about the issues of life and history. That was how I got most of my family information. I asked him, "Papa, why is it that you never display anger?" My dad smiled ruefully and answered softly, "I can, and I do display anger, however, if and when I become angry, I can be very destructive and would remain implacable for several days. Therefore, *I chose* never to be angry anymore in my life."

Reverend Joel Osteen, the pastor at Lakewood Church in Houston, Texas, said in a sermon, "When you let people upset you, you are giving away your power; you are letting him control you. If they push certain buttons and you get offended, and they bait you into a conflict, why don't you turn those buttons off? Life is so much free when you are not controlled by what people say or do ... you are not sour when traffic gets delayed, you are not bitter when someone takes up your parking lot, or insults you.... You retain your calm and your joy. Don't you take the bait. You do not let them empty the garbage they are carrying onto your head.

But suppose they dump their garbage on you, do not make the mistake of getting upset, otherwise you will be carrying their garbage. Sooner or later, you will dump it on someone else. Do not take it personally because it has nothing to do with you. Instead, smile, wish them well and move on. Successful people do not let garbage dumping overtake their day, or influence the course of their events."

You would have thought that Joel met Ezekiel – that is, Pastor Joel met Chief Ezekiel Ade Ajayi, (my dad) because what the pastor said in 2020 was what my dad did in 1962.

Like my father did in his time, you can train yourself to not rise to any bait. You can choose to master and exercise self-control. The Lord taught us well in asking us not to repay evil for evil, to absorb wrongs, and move on, even to seek peace and *pursue* it. He that will pursue peace does not lose self-control. He waits for the mud to dry before he attempts to wipe it off. Else he makes matters worse by wiping the mud when it is still fresh!
He *pursues* peace. '*Pursue'* is an active word that implies a deliberate act; a search for peace. That's what Christians are advised to do. That was what Christ did. A true Christian seeks peace and actively PURSUES, chases after, it. If you do, PTL (Praise the Lord).

200   THE BLESSINGS OF SELF-CONTROL #16

One Wednesday morning in 2001, at about 10:30 in the morning, midway through my surgical list, I was told that the Hospital authorities had stopped my next patient from coming into the operating theatre. I had finished an operation, and usually, we would send for the next patient when I gave the signal that the preceding case was finishing successfully. In between, we surgeons would nip into the recess room for coffee or a phone call to a dear one or visit the bathroom. My patient had completed all pre-operative protocols – seen in the clinic, treated unsuccessfully by medications, agreed to surgery as the definitive treatment modality, understood the proposed procedure, had given implicit consent, had signed a piece of paper called the *Consent Form*, had been fasting since midnight and been admitted as an inpatient earlier. But a non-medically-trained personnel was obstructing me – and, as I was to discover later, – legally!

It transpired that a man had been brought to the Accident and Emergency Department by an ambulance, and the attending doctors had correctly diagnosed a life-threatening condition that would take his life if urgent (and major) surgery was not performed. The condition was a "leaking aneurysm", that is, a major blood vessel has developed a defect whereby its wall was overstretched and has ballooned out. At the maximum point of stretch, it had ruptured slightly and started to bleed. Without prompt treatment, he would bleed to death in a matter of hours. Hypertension is a common cause, although other reasons like inborn weakness of the blood vessel wall could be responsible. As hospital protocols go, the next available surgical operating table shall be made available for the life-saving surgical operation that the patient needs. On that day, I was the surgeon who would finish earliest of the many ongoing simultaneous operations. My table was going to be the first available.

The Lord Jesus Christ taught his followers to try and practise self-control. We are not supposed to rise to every bait, get angry, seek revenge or be bitter. Disappointments might even be God's design to usher us into what he had planned for us (Gen. 45, 5, 8; Jer 29:11).

Scientists have long discovered that people who have anger or bitterness may produce an excess of certain hormones called catecholamines(*adrenaline* and *noradrenaline*) from their adrenal glands. One gland is situated just above each kidney. Adrenaline and noradrenaline cause the walls of arterial blood vessels to contract during stress and get us ready for a *fight, flight or fright reaction.* They squeeze blood toward the heart. This increases the pressure in the heart. In other words, the blood pressure rises. Increased blood pressure is called *hypertension*. Prolonged untreated hypertension may cause many harmful conditions in our body, such as:

1. Heart attack;
2. Stroke (bleeding into the brain or haemorrahgic stroke. The commoner form of stroke is thrombotic – from a blood clot);
3. Aneurysm – the wall of the blood vessel thins and balloons out
4. Heart failure – weak heart
5. Weakened and narrowed blood vessels in the kidneys
6. Thickened, narrowed or torn blood vessels in the eyes
7. Trouble with memory or understanding leading to dementia.

It pays us to listen to what Christ taught us so that we may "live abundantly" rather than allow pride, disobedience and bitterness to shorten our lives. If anger causes our blood pressure to rise to the extent that we bleed into our brain (stroke), we only will suffer the disability that such a condition brings. It is, therefore, a thing for which to praise the Lord if we could but exercise self–control.

201. For giving us the blessing of sleep
202. For a bed to sleep upon
203. And watching over us during our sleep[4]
204. For giving us the ability to dream in our sleep
205. For dreams that warn us of our behaviours
206. For the twenty and four elders that surround His throne
207. For His innumerable company of angels
208. For the ministry of angels
209. For human beings in our lives who do the work of angels

---

[4] Remarkably, we tend not to choke on our saliva or swallow our tongue whilst we are asleep.

201 SLEEP – 1 #17

Sleep is nature's way to refresh our body and mind after each day's exertion. Children fall asleep easily and can be unconcerned in a noisy environment. Adults, however, sleep for less as they grow older and often need a quiet ambience to fall and stay asleep. As the cares of the world and our responsibilities increase, our sleep is disturbed. Some people may use medications to help them fall asleep, but these will stop being effective after a while. A good night's sleep is God's gift to man. Many of us even have our own beds and can choose when we sink into bed and when we get out of it: prisoners don't have that luxury! Soldiers, too, might not be so indulged whilst on active service.

When we sleep, we are often oblivious to whatever might be going on around us. Wicked people could take advantage of this non-awareness to break into our house, our room, or, in some instances, carry out a sexual assault.

Our muscles relax so much that it would be possible to 'swallow our tongue' in our sleep, thereby causing airway obstruction and death. However, this is very rare – not because we know what to do, but because of God's providence. If we accidentally slept on one side all night, we could obstruct blood flow to our legs and then wake up with temporary paralysis in the leg. Thus, we have the instinct to turn in bed periodically at night and thus, restore blood flow to our limbs as well as relieve an unintended blockage of our airways.

209 ANGELS IN HUMAN CLOTHING – 1 #18

When we pray for God's help, most of our assistance comes from humans who God has sent to help us.
A true story comes from Kenya:
A woman died during childbirth, but the baby survived. Her husband blamed the new baby son for killing his wife and disowned him. The boy grew up in the streets and became a beggar. One day he spotted a woman in the back of a car and was moved with pity for the woman who had some breathing difficulty and was attached to a few tubes. The boy instinctively gave his takings to the woman because he felt that she needed it more than him. He might be poor, but he was rich in health and compassion. The sick woman publicised the encounter, and people rallied around to pay her hospital bills. One of them, another woman, went one step further – she adopted the orphan boy and sent him to school. She was his angel!

Praise Him for His names which include:

210. The Ancient of days (Dan 7:9)
211. The I am; the I am that I am (Exo 3:14)
212. God of gods (Daniel 2:47)
213. The Holy One (Lev 11:44)
214. The Lifter up of our heads (Ps 3:3)
215. The King of Nations (Jer 10:7)
216. The Fountain of Living Waters (Jer 2:13)
217. The Great I am (Ex 3:14)
218. The Lord of Hosts (Hag 2:4, 7, 8, 9.)
219. The Lord, the God of all flesh (Jer 32:27)
220. The Highest (Ps 18:13)
221. The Lord is His name (Amos 5:8)
222. The Lord Our **Provider** (Jehovah Jireh; Adonai-Jireh: Gen 22:13-14)

223. The Lord Our **Healer** (Jehovah Ropheka; Rapha - Exo 15:26)
224. The Lord Our **Righteousness** (Jehovah **Tsikenu** - Jer 23:6)
225. The Lord Our **Banner** (Jehovah Adonai – Nissi; - Exo 17:8-15)
226. The Lord Our **Peace** (Jehovah Shalom - Judges 6:24)
227. The Lord My **Shepherd** (Jehovah Ro'I - Psa 23:1)
228. The Lord Is **Present** (Adonai-**Shammah** - Ezek 48:35)

GOD – HIS ATTRIBUTES

God, You are

229. Abounding in mercy
230. Abounding in love (Ps 103:8)
231. Ageless
232. Alive; The Living God
233. Almighty
234. Amazing
235. All-sustaining
236. Almighty
237. Authoritative
238. Awe-inspiring
239. Beautiful
240. Blessed for Evermore
241. Benevolent
242. Caring
243. Clever
244. Compassionate (Psalm 145:8)
245. Consistently good
246. Constant
247. Covenant-keeping God (2Chr. 14)
248. Creative
249. Dependable
250. Divine

251. Endless
252. Eternal
253. Everlasting
254. Ever-present in times of trouble
255. Excellent (Ps 8:1)
256. Extraordinary
257. Fair
258. Faithful[5]
259. Fatherly
260. Forbearing
261. Forgiving
262. Generous
263. God
264. Good (Ps 118:1; Ps 119:68; Ps 135:3; Ps 145:9; Nahum 1:7)
265. The Lord is good and doeth good (Ps 119:68)
266. Glorious
267. Gracious (Ps 145:8)
268. Great (Ps 135:5)
269. Helpful
270. Holy
271. Infinite
272. Immutable (Ps. 102:27) - unchanging
273. Impartial
274. Impeccable
275. Imperious
276. Incomparable
277. Infallible
278. Infinite
279. Inimitable
280. Inscrutable
281. Intelligent
282. Invincible
283. Invisible
284. Jehovah

---

[5] See *Faithfulness of God, p102*

285. Just
286. Kind
287. Knowledgeable
288. Limitless
289. Longsuffering
290. Lord God
291. Love
292. Loving
293. Majestic
294. Merciful (Jer. 3:12)
295. Magnificent
296. Marvellous (Ps 98:1)
297. Matchless
298. Meticulous
299. Mighty
300. Mindful of men,
301. Miracle Worker
302. New in mercy every day,
303. Non-discriminatory
304. No respecter of persons
305. Omni-helpful
306. Omni-loving (all-loving)
307. Omni-merciful
308. Omni-perfect
309. Omnipotent
310. Omnipresent
311. Omniscient
312. Omni-watchful
313. One
314. Our Father in Heaven
315. Our God   (2Chr 13:10)
316. Paramount
317. Peerless
318. Perfect in all His ways
319. Powerful
320. Praiseworthy
321. Preeminent

322. Promise-keeping
323. Propitious
324. Provident – cares and provides
325. Pure
326. Quality but not quantity-inclined
327. Real
328. Reliable
329. Responsible
330. Righteous Father (Ps 12:7; Ps 98; Ps 129:4; John 17: 25)
331. Sagacious
332. Sinless
333. Slow to anger
334. Sovereign
335. Spirit
336. Steadfast in love
337. Strong
338. Sublime
339. Super
340. Superb
341. Superlatively wise
342. Supreme
343. The Fountain of Life
344. Fountain of Living
345. The God of all the Earth
346. The God of Heaven
347. The God of Peace
348. The God who spoke by the prophets (Hebrews 1:1)
349. The God who spoke by the prophets and multiplied visions (Hosea 12:9-10)
350. The Great I am
351. The King of Glory (Ps 24: 10)
352. The King of Heaven (Dan 4:37)
353. The Lifter up of our head
354. The Living God
355. The Lord Our Righteousness (Jer. 23:6)
356. The Lord that answers by Fire (1 Kings 18:38)
357. The Lord who is slow to anger

358. The Lord who will not acquit the wicked (Nahum. 1:3)
359. The Lord in whom there is no unrighteousness (Psalm, 92:15)
360. The Lord in whom there is no variableness (James 1:17); and,
361. There is no shadow of turning with God (ibid)
362. The Lord who rebukes the sea and dries it up
363. The Most High God
364. The Only God
365. The only Potentate (1 Tim 6:15)
366. The Source of all good things
367. Tender
368. Thorough
369. Timeless
370. Ultimate
371. Unblamable
372. Unchangeable
373. Unchanging
374. Understanding
375. Unique
376. Unlimited
377. Unparalleled
378. Unquestionable
379. Venerable
380. Venerated
381. Victorious
382. Watchful
383. Way Maker (Isaiah 43:19)
384. Wisdom personified
385. Wise
386. Without compare
387. Wonderful
388. Worthy
389. Yahweh
390. Zealous (Ex 34:14)

#285 PUNISHING THE RIGHTEOUS WITH THE WICKED - God is Just. Story no. 19

My headteacher at St, Michael's, Ikole-Ekiti, Mr Odupaye, was making his announcements before he dismissed the pupils at the close of day in 1967. "Every student must bring two stakes of bamboo tomorrow for the construction of the school fence. We need to ward off goats and sheep from the garden." He had barely finished when his deputy, Mr Omole, took to the lectern and announced that each pupil must bring four and not two. A voice was heard from a student, "Bastard." Mr Omole heard the swearing made by a student who had felt that the vice principal was inconsiderate.

"Who called me a bastard?"
The room fell silent. There was no taker, not surprisingly. The livid teacher repeated his question, but everybody in the assembly hall was mute. We waited with bated breath ...

Not content to let a delinquent stripling get away with rudeness to an elder, he vowed to beat the devil out of a segment of pupils from where he thought he heard the voice. Everybody remained silent, so he replayed the sound in his head and picked out Segun, one year older than me but slightly of a smaller frame with not much flesh or fatty tissue to cushion the force of the incipient strokes that would soon tattoo his backside. Segun confidently averred that he knew the culprit: Omoniyi. And for good measure to prove his innocence, he started sobbing uncontrollably as the wronged party. His antics worked. Omoniyi, who was physically bigger than Segun and, in appearance, more rustic, denied that he was the culprit. No matter, he was hauled out, and four burly boys held him down while our teacher administered six strokes of his cane. Segun and I trekked home in the same company that afternoon. When Omoniyi's company had turned off at a road junction, I broke the silence by asking Segun if he truly was guilty. He confessed that the word slipped out of his mouth and did not realize it was audible. He feared for his life, so he put up a performance to prove his innocence! It was then obvious that Omoniyi was flogged for a sin he did not commit!

Miscarriage of justice still happens today, resulting in wrongful state-sanctioned executions, imprisonments, ruinous litigations, broken marriages, children taken into care and the ruining of good friendly relationships. Only God is a true and just judge, and for His impartiality and thoroughness, we ought always to praise the Lord.[6] (See the Patricia Stalling Story p91).

332 SLOW TO ANGER 20

In my youth, when I was a choirboy in my home church at Ikole-Ekiti, the choirmaster composed an anthem for the church. The lyrics included lines like

"It is the man that is angry; If God were angry, who would be unaffected?
"It is a man that avenges; if God chose to avenge, who would stand?
"It is man that judges, if God were to judge, who would be guiltless?"

If we consider our ways, and God metes out instant judgement, hardly any living soul will be accounted innocent. The year 2020 showed the darker side of man, the brutality displayed by the American policemen towards suspected lawbreakers made the jaw

---

[6] See **The Patricia Stalling Story p91**

drop. The extra-judicial killing of men of certain races left a lot to be desired; the wanton killing of certain minority tribes in Nigeria was atrocious. The displacement of some people in Burma because of their race and faith bordered on the callous. The misappropriation of large sums of money by politicians in low-resourced countries that left the poor sections of their societies in poverty and hunger was inhumane. Elsewhere in the world, there was human trafficking; traffickers put refugees on flimsy inflatable dinghies across treacherous waters that took the lives of a lot of these people who were fleeing poverty and have paid large sums of money to intermediaries and people smugglers. There were extortionate natives of certain countries that these refugees had to pass through and who captured the migrants and used them as unpaid servants or physically abused them. There were rapists and sexual abusers who humiliated women. There were internet fraudsters who shamelessly and coldly fleeced people of their life savings, or, caused large corporations to divert to their accounts money that was meant to pay for services between companies. There were people who hid under the guise of religion to gather and deceive congregants; they indoctrinated, brainwashed and fleeced them of their money by a combination of wrongful interpretation of Scripture and the doctrine of fear; and many more. Yet, we serve a patient God who is not only VERY slow to anger but quite forgiving. He waits patiently and gives several opportunities for the sinner to repent; for the prodigal to come home, for the wayward to correct his ways. If God metes out instant judgement, not many of us will remain on God's earth.

For the Almighty's patience, we have cause to thank and to praise the Lord.

AND, WE PRAISE YOU BECAUSE YOU ARE OUR

391. Buckler (Ps 18:2)
392. Bulwark
393. Defence
394. Deliverer (Ps 18:2)
395. Ebenezer
396. Fortress (Ps 18:2; 31:3; 91:2;)
397. Help and our shield (Ps 33:20)
398. Hiding Place (Ps 32:7)
399. High Tower
400. Hope
401. Light (Ps 27:1)
402. Rock (Deut. 32:15; Ps 18:2; 31:3)
403. Shepherd (Ps 23:1)
404. Shield
405. Strength (Ps 18:2)
406. The Horn of our salvation (Ps 18:2)
407. We thank You because some people depend on us
408. For those on whom we, in turn, depend
409. For all who contributed to our upbringing
410. For our Dad
411. Our Mum
412. Siblings to grow up with
413. Grandparents
414. For our children and grandchildren
415. For causing our dads to meet our mums
416. For being conceived
417. For being born alive

395 THE LORD IS OUR EBENEZER #21

Every year, most of us mark our birthdays. Some hold parties, and some go on holidays, ocean cruises, hold thanksgiving services in churches or arrange donations to charitable causes. At other times, we gain promotion at work or get elected to high office as politicians, administrators or managers of business corporations. Then, there is a celebration for childbirth, recovery from illness, purchasing a house, marriage and close escape from accidents. Sometimes a country comes through a war, famine, or natural disaster. Each of these calls for celebrations and an acknowledgement of God's grace and bounty.

In ancient Israel, there was a time that the people stopped to thank God:
The Israelites had brought the Ark of the Covenant to Kirjath Jearim and kept it there for twenty years. The prophet Samuel gathered the people together to fast and pray. The Philistines went up against them to fight, but the Israelites cried unto God for Help. The Lord confounded the Philistines with thunder and scattered the enemy. Israel pursued them and won a great victory. As a testimony to God's intervention, Samuel erected the "Stone of Help" – Ebenezer – meaning, "Hitherto hath the Lord helped us." 1 Sam 7:12

We, too, can say 'Ebenezer' for such times in our lives when the Lord has won important victories for us because the Lord is our Help.

417 BEING BORN ALIVE 22

Every human being that we meet is a walking miracle. Conception is not a given or automatic process – ask infertile couples – and being pregnant does not automatically guarantee that the woman will take a baby home at the end of her pregnancy. Conception does not equate to a baby. Of all known cases of pregnancies, about 1 in 5 (20%) are lost to miscarriage. If we consider all fertilisations and early "chemical" pregnancies[7], then, it is said that about 70% or 7 in 10 conceptions miscarry. If you observe an apple or mango tree at the end of Spring, you will notice many fruits falling off the trees – wasted. Most of such discarded fruits appear normal to the naked eye. Human pregnancy is just like those whereby 'normal' fetuses are miscarried. Sometimes the miscarriage is due to chromosomal abnormalities such as excess or paucity of chromosomes. When cells divide during the making of eggs (spermatogenesis or oophogenesis), human cells divide perfectly into two halves, each containing 23 genetic units (chromosomes). Any slight mistake that causes one egg to have 22 (one fewer) or 24 (one too many) will result in fetal abnormality. Often these are lethal, and the fertilized egg is naturally miscarried. Miscarriage and the severity of abnormality depend on which pair of chromosomes contain the extra chromosome. The 46 chromosomes of a human cell are paired up and numbered from the largest to the smallest. Pair number one is the largest, and the smallest is number 22. The 23rd pair is the sex chromosomes.

If the extra chromosome is on any pair (making three – or *trisomy*), it is lethal and incompatible with survival except, occasionally, when the extra chromosome is on the 21st pair. That is the only instance

---

[7] *A chemical pregnancy is one where a routine pregnancy test is positive for the hormone of pregnancy, but there is no physical evidence of a developing pregnancy. Such pregnancies last for only a few hours or a few days. They are the very early miscarriages.*

when trisomy (three chromosomes in a "pair") is compatible with life. The condition is called Trisomy 21 or, more popularly, Down's Syndrome, and we all know that children affected by this condition have a few abnormalities and many life challenges. Medical literature lists some of the effects from reduced mental awareness to slanting eyes and a tongue that appears rather large for the mouth. The way the eye slants gave rise to one of the older names of the syndrome: '*Mongolism*,' after the eye features of an Eastern race. Much rarer trisomies occur in pairs number 13 and 18. Babies born with these abnormalities rarely survive to birth, or if born alive, they tend to have a very short life span, with quite a lot of disabilities.

If one chromosome was absent, the child conceived has one less sex chromosome than normal. Hence, instead of a normal complement of 46 chromosomes (44xx or 44xy), she has 45 (44xo). That is Turner's Syndrome. All are girls. The girl will typically have a short stature, widely-spaced nipples, a webbed neck, underdeveloped internal reproductive organs and a potentially fatal condition where the largest artery in the human body, the aorta, is narrowed near the heart (coarctation). She does not have egg-making capabilities and, scientifically speaking, cannot be a mother. The womb (uterus) is also not well developed. Hormones exist in the hands of specialists to help such girls add a bit to their stature to minimize social embarrassment from unknowing, curious neighbours and schoolmates.

Other than chromosomal abnormalities of trisomy and monosomy, infections, trauma, radiation, drugs, febrile illness, and a weakened neck of the womb (cervical incompetence) can cause a miscarriage. Nevertheless, all these account for only about half of miscarriages. In the other half, doctors have no clue about what causes miscarriage. We call those '*idiopathic*' – of unknown cause. Therefore, for our mothers to conceive and give birth to us is a miracle that we – or the mums – have no control over. Being born alive is a big reason to

thank God whenever we remember our births and mark our birthdays.
(Issues causing pregnancy loss in the latter half of pregnancy are discussed in Chapter 4 under Reproduction).

418. For being born alive and wanted[8]
419. Or, if abandoned, for providing carers and foster parents to raise us[9]
420. For being born free.

420 BORN FREE – Of Slaves, Low Castes and Indentured Servants. 23

ONE OF THE GREATEST PRIVILEGES OF OUR LIVES IS that we were born free. If you had your parents, grew up in your own home, were free to play in the neighbourhood, grow and develop under favourable conditions, you have a lot to be thankful for always.

Imagine indentured servants. They grow up to realize that their parents have borrowed money from rich neighbours and sent a child to work to repay the debt. They cannot go to school, nor can they

---

[8] some babies are abandoned in trash bins: it easily could have been us!

[9] Quite a few of us know one or more people who were brought up by kind foster parents.

participate in ordinary childhood pastimes. The practice still exists in certain countries in the 21st century!

A practice worse than being indentured is slavery. A slave is owned, and there is no agreed day to set him free. He cannot choose when to sleep or what to eat. He is assigned work that a natural parent would consider excessive. He is a property, a "thing" to be used, a commodity that can be traded, and an accessory that can be discarded anyhow, anytime. His opinion is never sought. He cannot answer back, cannot refuse abuse, challenge an infringement on his rights, or question cruelty. He cannot take food thrown away at the risk of being beaten, sometimes to death. His lips, ears, face, forehead or body can be branded with a searing hot iron with the initials of his master owner. He was once used unethically for scientific experiments such as "The Tuskegee Study of Untreated Syphilis in the Negro Male" in America between 1932 and 1972. He has no status, rights or standing. He is not allowed to reproduce or enjoy sensual pleasures. If female, she could be used for the sexual pleasure of the owner or any of his sons. He may not complain of illness or tiredness. He is taken away from his people, who he might never see again in life (Remember the minstrel song, *Old Folks at Home: Way Down the Swanee River* by Stephen Foster in 1851 America where a young lad was lamenting and wondering if he would ever see his mother and brother again?). A slave is given a new culture, a new name, a new identity in a new and alien environment. He could be sold with no prior warning. If ever he bears children, or the female slave becomes pregnant, even for her master, her children automatically become slaves and swell the numbers. All his work is never paid for – they are free, for the master; 'enforced' *pro bono* work. His labour, in the prime of his life, is never allowed to benefit the land of his birth, rather, it goes to develop other people's lands and economy. They prosper while his own people are impoverished. He labours to grow his master's family and business but he has none of his own. His generations after him bear the stigma of being slaves. If manumission occurs, his offspring are denied political office, access to services and privileges, and relegated to the very bottom rung of the ladder. It is then a lifelong struggle to rise from those doldrums. Even so, his achievements are derided, pooh-poohed and sabotaged. Genuine contributions are overlooked or conveniently ignored. Worse, as he grows up, long after his freedom, the generations of his abusers disdain his generation after him and call them "backward," because they conveniently forget that they were instrumental to his plight.

Of all inhumanity of man against man, slavery is the worst. It removes humanity, strips the slave of dignity and human-ness. When a slave regains freedom, his best days are behind him, and he has to strive extra hard to keep his head above the waters. He is a second-class citizen because most of his neighbours belong to the same stock as his master and have the same mentality. He must still live in fear, in enforced civility and stoop, at all times, to be allowed to carry out business. If his house was vandalised, he might not complain because that might attract opprobrium and revenge attacks. He cannot hope for justice, for justice might mean accusing persons of higher social strata.

Therefore, if anyone is not a slave or belongs to the low caste peoples of countries that practise that despicable custom, they should be thankful to the Lord. If you have **never** experienced the feeling of being cast in the role of a slave, including being subjected to racism and similar treatment, you have reasons to praise the Lord.

421. For the midwives who cared for my mother on the day that I was born
422. For helping me escape childhood diseases
423. For the childhood immunizations that prevented infections[10]

---

[10] Children receive various vaccinations: measles, mumps, rubella, pertussis, and polio, amongst others.

424. Making me escape childhood accidents, abusers and kidnappers.

424 DISSIPATING ACCIDENTS – part 1, note 24

IN MY FIRST YEAR as an intern, I was invited to a birthday party by a young student nurse. Her brother, the pastor of a small congregation church, proposed her toast, during which he related an experience in his childhood days. He was about to travel from his home city of Owo to Lagos in Nigeria. The practice was that passengers took their seats on the bus on a first-come, first-served basis. Some elderly folk who joined late might be honoured by a younger person who would voluntarily give up his choice seat out of cultural respect, but this was never enforced except on that day. The young man had arrived early and taken his seat beside the driver, having a clear view of the road ahead. When the last seat had been taken, and the driver was about to start off, an older man came along. Finding no space and with a sense of entitlement, he came alongside the front passenger's seat and ordered the boy out of the bus. Angry, sad and feeling cheated, the lad disembarked and swallowed hard at the injustice and brazen robbery. If any adult intervened, it fell upon deaf ears.

Later that night, news filtered into town that the bus had crashed along its route without any survivors. The conclusion was stark: he would not have lived to see his sister's twenty-first birthday.

For every air crash, every rail derailment, every holiday coach tumbling down a hill, there is probably somebody who missed their trip because of some delay: lost tickets, traffic delay on the way to the airport, refusal by immigration officials to allow boarding or, oversleeping and being late in arriving at the departure lounge.

Those who die in accidents are not necessarily worse sinners than those who escape death. For survivors, every additional day that we get to spend on earth is a gift from God.

Sometimes, whilst driving, people cut across us or ask to be given the right of way. We might stop for a pedestrian, an elderly lady or an animal to cross the road despite running late. Such acts might delay us for up to one minute. However, **a delay of a single second is all it takes to help us escape some accidents.** If we were driving along a road at 30 miles per hour, we were, in essence, covering 30 miles in 60 minutes. That equates to one mile every 2 minutes, or 1,760 yards every two minutes (120 seconds). That is 880 yards every 60 seconds or 14 yards every second. That is three car lengths every second. Now, think about this: most car accidents, head-on collisions, and crashes could easily be avoided if the car had been 14 yards slower or faster.

There was a freak storm in England on 19 February 2022. His car was hit by a flying debris during *Storm Eunice*. A solo second slower or faster would have meant the debris missed him – remember FOURTEEN YARDS is three car lengths?

Therefore, the next time you travel in a car, think of the many accidents that could have happened – but for the grace of God.
Go on, praise the Lord!

424/2 DISSIPATING ACCIDENTS – part 2, #25

On September 26 1992, a plane carrying 151 military officers and eight crew members went down in a swamp at Ejigbo, near Lagos, Nigeria. The Lockheed C-130H Hercules was carrying the servicemen back to their command in the northern city of Kaduna, about 800 miles away. There was not a single survivor.
The plane had taken off three minutes earlier from the Murtala Mohammed Airport in Lagos and crashed after three of its four engines failed one after the other. After the first engine failed, the pilot was not overly concerned as three could get the plane to its destination, but after the second failed, he made a U-turn to return to the airport. By the time the third failed, he was quoted as admitting that they would not make it to the airport. He had the clarity of thought to put the plane down in a swamp, away from residential areas to minimize civilian casualty. Conspiracy theories sprang up, amongst which was that it was sabotage engineered by someone who wanted the military personnel dead.

On September 26 2020, one of my medical school classmates who joined the army straight out of university wrote on our class forum how he was grateful to God that he did not die that day. Andy ought to have been aboard the plane, but for the simple reason that he chose to spend a few more days in Lagos to be beside his wife as she gave birth to their baby in the Lagos University Teaching Hospital. Today, Andy has retired at the statutory age for officers in his cadre and describes himself as *"retired but refired* for God."

A friend told a similar story on March 2 2021. 'CT' was writing a comment under a mutual friend's Facebook post and gave his testimony which was similar to Andy's:

"On one occasion, my refusal to bribe airline officials saved my life. The staff at a Nigeria Airways plane checking-in counter demanded bribes from me, but I refused flatly. We were bound for Enugu. The ground staff of the then corrupt Nigeria Airways wanted just 1,000 naira (about £5 then)) but I bluntly refused because I knew I had a boarding card to and from Enugu airport. As my punishment, my seat was taken away from me and given to the wife of then governor of Anambra State, Mrs J.N. The plane took off without me but crashed at Enugu Airport as it was attempting to land.

"That was a Monday. Two days later (Wednesday), I travelled to Enugu and saw the plane where it had crashed in the vicinity of the airport. My integrity saved me. God kept me from harm."

The first story was Andy's and the second, Christopher's, but who knows how many times in our lives that God had used a family event, a delay, a lack, an obstacle, a call to help someone, a minor illness, a missed train, a lost car key, a quarrel with our spouse and such like, to "deliver us from evil"? Even if we cannot identify specific occasions, we must trust in the goodness of the Lord to do this for us many times, and therefore, praise the Lord.

425. Restoration of those with traumatic childhood experiences
426. Helping me to attend school and be educated and instructed
427. Providing enough money for my parents to pay for my education
428. Helping me gain admission to schools
429. Helping me pass my examinations
430. Helping that my examination papers were not misplaced
431. Making me healthy enough to complete my education
432. Helping me graduate from each school – primary, secondary and university
433. For the teachers who shaped my knowledge
434. For friends that I made at school
435. Being able to read

436. For schoolmates who played with me and taught me friendship values
437. For those who disappointed me and thereby taught me valuable lessons of life
438. For helping me keep most of my childhood friends
439. For those who still care for me, pray for me, advise me and visit me
440. Giving me enough nutrition as I grew up
441. Helping me to feel hunger and so appreciate those who struggle for daily bread
442. For enabling me to grow up in peacetime – some saw World Wars 1 & 2.
443. For our friends
444. For our relatives
445. For those who have died and left a good legacy
446. For community, neighbourhood and townspeople
447. For guidance, angels, messenger angels and helpful angels
448. For the twenty and four elders that surround God's throne

.... **GOD's WORKS:**

449. For His works are mighty, miraculous and uncountable;
450. His ways are past finding out
451. His mercies endure forever
452. Performed wonders in the land of Egypt
453. Saved His people by His outstretched right hand
454. He led the patriarchs through the wilderness
455. Guided them by the pillars of Cloud and of Fire
456. Fed them with Manna, the bread of heaven
457. Assuaged their thirst in the desert
458. Gave them water from the Rock
459. Gave them the laws and the commandments

460. Healed their diseases
461. Protected them from enemy attacks
462. Miraculously helped them to cross the Red Sea
463. And the River Jordan (Joshua 3)
464. Appointed leaders for them
465. And preserved their heritage
466. He guided them safely to The Promised Land
467. And gave them portions of land to settle on
468. Gave them Judges, Kings, Prophets and Priests
469. Made His ways and His preferences known to them
470. And taught the fathers who taught their children
471. Established His name amongst them.
472. Chose us
473. Made us joint heirs of the heavenly promise
474. He gave us favour (Proverbs 8:35)
475. Has only thoughts of peace towards us, to give us an expected end (Jer 29:11)
476. And making us receive the favour of the Lord (Luke 1:43)
477. For making us believe what God said would be accomplished (Lk 1:45)
478. Gave us names whilst we were yet unborn (Isaiah 49:2)
479. He took us out of our mother's womb (Ps 22:9)
480. Calms the storms of life (Jonah 1:15)
481. Rides upon the storm (Ps29:10)
482. He sits upon the circle of the earth
483. Daily loads us with benefits
484. Makes us lie in the green pasture
485. Restores our souls (Ps 23:3)
486. Leads us in the path of righteousness (23:3)
487. The Lord is with us (23:4)
488. The Lord anoints our head with oil (23:8)
489. Watches over us day by day.

208 & 489 ANGELS IN HUMAN CLOTHING (2):
MINISTRY OF ANGELS - IN NIGERIA? 26

Deep in the heart of Nigeria when the jungle was still so thick as to encroach on roads and encounters with wild cats and other beasts were more than mere legends, a missionary experienced "angels hovering round" as the lyrics of a worship song in 1843, "A Friend's hymnal" stated. The gripping story was narrated by a woman missionary to my home state of Ekiti, in Western Nigeria, Miss Sheilagh Jebb. Her father, the Reverend Charles William Jebb, had been a Church Missionary Society (CMS) clergyman in Ekiti, Akoko and Owo about seven years before the outbreak of the First World War. Arriving at Lagos in 1907, aged 29, he was posted to Ado-Ekiti, where Reverend Tom Harding was the pioneer missionary.

Rev. Jebb would go back to England on holidays where he got married. In 1923, his second baby, Sheilagh arrived. She went to school and trained as a nurse in England but wanted to be a missionary. At Owo, my father, Chief E Ade Ajayi, lived with Reverend Jebb as a page boy with three other striplings while they attended elementary (Standard) school. The stories he told me about Reverend Jebb caused me to trace his family when I arrived in England in 1984. However, it was not until 2016, when I went to work in Belfast, that I heard of Miss Jebb's autobiographical book, "*Going For God*," in which she told this remarkable story.

A village chief had dispatched two men to go and fetch Reverend Tom Harding because he wanted to hear what he was preaching. Until then, he had been hostile to the gospel message, had forbidden his subjects from welcoming the white missionary and had insisted on worshipping his traditional gods. Reverend Harding requested the younger missionary, Jebb, to accompany him to see the chief. Reverend Harding was old and walked slowly, so he asked Revd Jebb to walk ahead with one of the men, and he followed behind with the older villager as his companion. Along the way, Reverend Jebb asked his companion how it was that the chief was now ready to see the Reverend Harding after his previous hostility. The villager related an astonishing story:

The man said, "I was one of the three best sharpshooters of bows and arrows who were sent by the chief six months ago to go and kill the old white man. When he came out among the banana trees, two things prevented us from shooting at him: there was another white man with him who kept getting in the way and we knew nothing of a second man, for you were not here then. Then there was something about that man that made us afraid, so we returned to the chief who was very angry that we had failed."

What transpired was that the chief had made further enquiries, and all he could hear were good reports about the white missionary, and he decided to hear Mr. Harding himself. That opened the way to proclaim the gospel to the whole village that night; people were converted and the first church was planted in the area.

Until Reverend Harding heard this story from Reverend Jebb, he was unaware of how close he came to death from a hostile native chief and how closer God had been to him, physically. It shows how God protects us – even if we don't thank Him, and with us being unaware! But it is always good to praise the Lord.

490. Neither sleeps nor winks.
491. Gives us our food in season
492. Helps us to control our appetite*
493. For the things we have and the positions we hold
494. Cares for us more than for the sparrow in the sky
495. Clothes us more than the flower of the field
496. Defends us from the accusation of Satan, our enemy
497. Protects and preserves us - from:

498. From falling trees
499. Landslides
500. Sinking grounds
501. Thunderbolts

492 BEING GRATEFUL FOR WHAT WE HAVE - 1
(For the things we have and positions we hold)

One common practice in humans is to focus on what we want rather than be grateful for what we have. Sometimes, a worker complains of being overworked and undervalued; he wants a promotion to the grade above him. However, for every salaried worker, there is an unemployed person who will happily step into his position.

I once came across a story of a man who owned a small car overtaking a limousine. He glanced at his rearview mirror and wondered if he could acquire such a luxury car. In that brief moment, he nearly ran over a biker. The biker accepted his apologies and thought to himself, "if only I had a car like this, I could travel without fear of the elements." As soon as the biker branched off the motorway, a man on a bicycle saw him on the other side of the road and admired his bike. He wished he owned a bike because going uphill would not be such a struggle. It was not long that a pedestrian sighed as his toes hurt on his trek. "Wouldn't it be nice to own a push-bike?" he intoned.

He soon reached the hospital where he was visiting an inpatient. As he waited for the lift, an older woman in a wheelchair joined the crowd gathering at the lifts. She admired the visitors and remembered the days when she walked without aid. She imagined how nice it was to porter around unaided. She soon reached her friend's bedside and became aware that she was more privileged than those patients who were not allowed out of bed. When she told her the ill friend to cheer up, the patient pointed out someone on life support who was in poorer shape than she was. A nurse attending the patient leaned forward, held the patient's hand and smiled, "I heard a woman praying earlier. But you know, I wasn't sure her husband heard her words. He is the man who has been on life support since March 13, four months now. She is always thanking God loudly that her husband is not in the morgue!"

492 BEING GRATEFUL FOR WHAT WE HAVE (but don't appreciate) – part 2, note 28.

In my university days, the students' Christian union met regularly in a big hall in the School of Nursing, a few hundred yards from the medical students' halls of residence. The female medical students' block was halfway between that of the student nurses and pupil midwives.

One evening as we gathered for our midweek meeting, one of my friends led the earlier part of the meeting. He requested somebody to lead the opening prayers and then specifically warned, "Not to thank God for water, air and such things ..." As those words rang out, there were gasps and a few words of dismay and disapproval, mainly from the female Christians. I felt slightly miffed at an oblique reference to me but pleased that some of our friends in the hall objected to what they thought was an incorrect call. My friend, leading the prayers on that occasion, had wanted someone who would pray a long prayer, spiced with quotes from the Bible and highfalutin names of God that serve only to impress the listeners. To him, the things that came to us easily – water, air, shelter, company, food, and the like – were nothing to thank God about. It is all too easy to take the simple things of life for granted and think that we do not owe God any gratitude for them.

The year 2020 taught the world that some people could not breathe as most of us can; the Ethiopian famine of the 1980s showed the world that if we have food, we ought to be grateful to God; the sailing crew in Samuel Taylor Coleridge's *Rhyme of the Ancient Mariner* told us that some people who are lost at sea, or facing drought, could and do die from thirst. In the past few years, many West African youths have tried to reach Europe by traversing the Sahara Desert in land vehicles. A survivor described the corpses that litter their path across the desert – antecessors who went before them with an inadequate water supply and who died of thirst. These people would appreciate the blessing of water.

Another blessing that we might take for granted is company. God had said. "It is not good for a man to be alone" in Genesis 2:18. During the first wave of Covid-19 lockdown in the United Kingdom, a pastor speaking to my church members online informed us there had been two cases of suicide in his church due to depression occasioned by loneliness in people living alone. Some of us can't stop arguing with our spouses, but it is still better to have someone to argue with than be lonesome. Along with activities that come to us with not much thought – like walking, swallowing and blinking, for example – we do not often thank God enough for people's company.

415 ESCAPING DEATH – 1 29th

It had rained heavily all day. In the evening after supper, the downpour had lessened but was still steadily persistent. In the boarding house of my grammar school, students had returned to their classes for evening study called "Preparation" or "prep" for short. But I was fascinated by the run-off water off my classroom roof, and I stood on the corridor facing our football field as I stuck my right hand out to catch rainwater. I enjoyed the feeling as the water ran off my fingers. All of a sudden, a humongous sinuous lightning lit the evening sky. Its dendrites went in all directions. Momentarily, the field and the horizon in front of me glowed in white. Instinctively, I knew that a large thunderbolt was coming. I tried to run indoors into my classroom, but the loud peal of the biggest thunder I had ever heard rang out. The building shook, and some students screamed. I knew that I had missed death by inches because it was apparent that trees nearby had been struck. I had jeopardized my life by offering myself as a lightning conductor, and not many men survive large voltages of such magnitude. I was shaking badly and couldn't sit alone. I went to sit near other students, where I felt slightly safe. Each time a smaller lightning flashed in the sky, my heart raced from fright. Back in our dormitory, I couldn't sleep alone in my bed and begged a student to let me shelter in his bed. I knew all night that I was moments away from being struck and electrocuted by a thunderbolt.

502. God protects us from foul air – carbon dioxide blanket[11]
503. Tsunamis
504. Earthquakes

---

[11] On August 21, 1986, many villagers in a town in Cameroon died after a lethal gas eruption from nearby Lake Nyos. Sensing the danger, some people tried to run away but died on the paths leading away from the town. It was believed that the offending gas was carbon dioxide which formed a blanket over the sleeping town. Animals and humans died in their sleep.

505. Volcanoes, floods, hurricanes,
506. Pandemics

424 SURVIVING DISASTERS – 1 30th

The coronavirus pandemic of 2020 taught man many lessons. Initially, they thought that the elderly were the susceptible ones. Some tropical African residents also boasted that the heat and perhaps the population's genetic composition were deterrents to the contagiousness of the virus. Eventually, as travel became unrestrained, every country was affected, including the young and warm climate dwellers. References and comparisons were made to the Spanish flu of 1919.

However, as happens with most natural disasters, some elderly folks survived whilst some youths died; Blacks died in their hundreds, especially in the United States of America. All races of all hues became casualties. There were severely affected individuals who beat the disease, and there were some in the prime of life who suddenly slumped and died before the symptoms were full-blown. Politicians and peasants, doctors and dockworkers, the rich and the ragged, all succumbed to the pandemic that did not discriminate for whom the bell tolled.

Science knew that some underlying medical illnesses predisposed sufferers to severe complications and death, but some people who had these survived, whereas healthy sportspersons did not fare well. Only God knew why some were spared – against all the odds – and some died. Some people who survived the viral disease were left with neurological deficits such as stroke, blindness and weakness in their limbs. Others had difficulty in breathing from fibrosed lungs and disorientation after coming out of an induced coma of several months. Several people had only the mild form of COVID-19, and tens of thousands never showed any symptoms though they tested positive for contracting the virus.

Whoever survived Covid-19 disease needs to thank the Lord!
Similarly, survivors of tsunamis, earthquakes, raging infernos, volcanoes, mudslides, tropical storms, sea and air accidents and wars have God to thank because family, relatives, neighbours, friends and foes do die from these disasters, while others live to tell the story.

491 SLEEP – 2: HELPING US TO CONTROL OUR APPETITE 31st

If we were left to our own devices, we would damage our health by our desires and appetites. One of my abiding memories in my early working life was seeing a toad overindulge itself. It was the rainy season in Akure, Nigeria. I was a junior doctor in the local hospital and had a hospital accommodation on the outskirts of town. It was a perfect setting for insects amidst the surrounding cornfields and fruit orchards. As happens after heavy rains and warm, humid evenings in the tropics, swarms of winged termites erupted from the anthills and swamped everything in the ambience. All manners of creatures swirled around to take advantage of nature's bounty. My two nieces who lived with us were amused as they pointed to a peculiar toad – it had eaten so much and had its stomach distended

to the extent that it lost its balance from a low tree branch, fell onto the ground and though the impact was mild its stomach burst.
The incident of a toad that overindulged makes me think of days when I had been deprived of sleep on night duty, and I would swear that once I was off duty, or on holiday, I would sleep for days on end. It never happened!

507. Will not suffer our soul to see corruption
508. Underneath us are His everlasting arms
509. Will not visit us with any of the diseases in Egypt (Ex 15:26)
510. Redeemed us (Ps. 31:5)
511. Considered our trouble (Ps 31:7)
512. Reassured us never to be afraid (Is 41:10)
513. Promised us His presence (Exo. 33:14)
514. Promised to help us (Is 41:10)
515. Helps the weak
516. Gives grace to the humble
517. Makes wise men foolish (in their imagination)
518. For allowing us to know just what is enough for us[12]
519. For giving every man AT LEAST something to be desired in them
520. For giving us courage, and a never-say-die attitude
521. For giving us the ability to express emotion
522. Promised never to forget us (Is 49:15)
523. Not given us over to our enemies

---

[12] There are things we know, and there are things that we don't. Deuteronomy 29:29 tells us that "the secret things belong to the Lord our God, but those things which are revealed belong to us and to our children forever, that we may do all the words of (God's) law." God permits us to know what is good for us. There are questions we and science may not be able to answer until we get to heaven.

524. Will not allow enemy's weapon to be effective against us (Is 54:17)
525. Set our feet upon the Rock
526. Prepared goodness for those who trust Him
527. Showed us His marvelous kindness
528. God uses affliction to work good in us (Ps 119:71; Is 48:10; Rom 8:28)
529. Will punish unrighteousness in future
530. He will not justify the sinner
531. Will not let the sinner go free[13]
532. The Lord is coming to judge the world in righteousness (Ps 98:9)
533. Will not punish the righteous with the wicked (Ezekiel 18:1-4; Genesis 18:24-26)

532 NOT PUNISHING THE INNOCENT – The Patricia Stallings' Story 32

At the end of each day, when we return home without any trouble with the outside world, we have reasons to thank God and praise His name. Many people are not usually so fortunate – some are accused of matters that they know nothing about, some are

---

[13] The human court system cannot be one hundred per cent accurate in determining all cases. In some instances, criminals engage clever attorneys and wriggle free of conviction, whereas failure to prove innocence might send an innocent accused to jail. Court systems might occasionally refuse evidence that could vindicate an accused person or convict the guilty if it meant that a case would be unduly prolonged or the evidence before the court appeared adequate. In such instances, justice could be misplaced.

accused of being in the wrong places at particular times, some walk into traps and some encounter situations that cannot easily be explained by simple logic and as such, they are held liable and accountable for any crime committed. Sometimes, innocuous, innocent statements get people into trouble. If such people were punished, we would say that they have suffered a miscarriage of justice. Ironically, judges and law enforcement personnel who mete out sentences mostly believe that they are acting right even if doubt exists, especially when a decision is made *on the balance of probability*. Worldwide, some prisoners ought not to be in jail but for the weakness and inflexibility of human law and the imperfection of human evidence. One of the worst cases of injustice that I have found was Mrs Patricia Stallings of St. Louis, USA. Wherever she is today, she almost certainly will be thanking God for intervening by a series of miraculous occurrences that freed her and taught humankind some lessons in judging cases. One of our prayers must always be *"Lead us not into temptation; but deliver us from evil,"* as Christ taught His disciples to pray.

Patricia Stallings
A mother failed by doctors, derided by lawyers, incarcerated by state but freed by God – for a crime she did not commit.

On July 9, 1989 in St Louis, Missouri, three-month-old Ryan Stallings became unwell. Parents Patricia and David rushed him to the hospital. Blood tests detected high levels of ethylene glycol, the main ingredient of antifreeze. Poisoning was suspected. Ryan responded to treatment, and upon discharge from the hospital, he was placed in protective care, despite protestations. On September 1, Patricia was permitted to visit her son briefly and under supervision. Three days later, on the 4th, baby Ryan fell ill again with excess ethylene glycol in his blood. He subsequently died.

The Stallings' house was searched and a half-empty gallon of antifreeze was found in the basement. Patricia was arrested and charged with murder which she strenuously denied. Her plea of natural causes was rejected, even ridiculed. Her husband, David, staunchly supported his wife and averred that she couldn't do it. She was sentenced to life without the possibility of parole.

In prison, Patricia discovered she had been pregnant at the time of her arrest. Elsewhere, experts were divided, but a professor of biochemistry at St Louis University, William Sly, posited that Ryan died of Methyl Malonic Acidaemia, MMA, rather than criminal poisoning. He was not believed.

As soon as Patricia gave birth in February 1990, the baby, named David Junior, was taken away to protective care. And although Patricia had no contact whatsoever with David Jnr, the tot fell ill – with excessive levels of ethylene glycol! The baby was then diagnosed *correctly* as suffering from ethylene glycol (MMA) in his blood. MMA is a rare genetic disorder where the body naturally produces supraphysiological levels of ethylene glycol. That was probably the condition that Ryan suffered from, and in retrospect, he must have died from natural causes! That line was pursued at appeal which was upheld.

Patricia was freed from jail – with apologies from the prosecutors – and David Jnr was returned to his parents in September 1991.

Where was God in all these? Why is it a reason to praise the Lord?

1. He granted that Patricia was pregnant before she was jailed;
2. Helped her husband to have faith in his wife's innocence to reduce her mental anguish;
3. Allowed baby David to suffer the same affliction as brother Ryan;

4. Helped that Patricia was not given leave to visit David around the time of his illness; and,
5. Permitted doctors to tie the two cases together to exonerate the babies' mothers.

If there had been no pre-sentencing pregnancy, or if David had not been born with MMA, Patricia in all probability would have died in prison with a mental breakdown as she would know that she was innocent and would have felt despondent that she couldn't prove her innocence in the courts of men. There certainly must be persons in our world today who suffer from crimes that they did not commit. The heart goes out to them. Such people are not necessarily worse than us; they are not greater sinners, but as the Preacher said, "*time and chance happen to us all.*" As you read this in the comfort of your home, you are not in jail, but you could have been! Therefore, let us thank the Lord.

530. NOT LETTING OFFENDERS/SINNERS GO FREE
33rd

I have a friend who once said that he would not serve or believe in a God who would forgive the South African White population who practised the Apartheid system that maltreated the native Black population for decades. The world witnessed the atrocities and the injustice of white domination of a people who originally inhabited the patch of land called South Africa. During a discussion, I mentioned that if the perpetrators of oppression and wickedness were to repent, God would forgive them. My friend thought that the unjust treatment meted to the blacks for several decades should not merit forgiveness by a just God! The Bible tells us otherwise – that no matter how terrible our sin is, our crimson-stained clothes can be washed clean if we come to God in repentance. God loves those who do right but, as humans tend to do evil spontaneously, He welcomes the penitent.

There are, however, acts of depravity and wickedness that go undetected because the perpetrator hides his deeds or operates under the cloak of darkness. The elderly get robbed and sometimes murdered; women get raped and left with long-lasting mental scars; certain priests reportedly sodomize young children, turning such innocents into mentally disturbed adults; rich people exercise power to deprive the poor of their land or means of sustenance; widows lose their inheritance to greedy and wicked relatives-in-law; government officials steal money budgeted to take care of the poor in society, and some university lecturers ask for sexual favours from their female students before allowing them to pass examinations or graduate. Also, kidnappers ask for huge ransom money in exchange for freeing their hapless victims; powerful governments undermine weaker ones to extract the latter's resources; sometimes, such powers remove leaders that appear to be too clever in leading their poor people out of bondage by the richer nations; some heads of state had been assassinated because their policy did not favour certain powerful nations with vested interests – in such cases, there is little consideration given to the women that were widowed or children that would be orphaned.

Elsewhere, a top official could be framed up by false evidence to force a resignation from office and in the process be humiliated by lies that he would be unable to disprove; a young girl might lie against an innocent man and accuse him of a serious sexual assault – many end up in jail for the sin they did not commit. It is not uncommon to notice that rich people lure desperate youths into slavery or that gangs force girls into prostitution just as dictators take out critics ostensibly to allow for the peace and progress of their nation's policies. These are some of the many sins that man commits, which might not be immediately apparent to any but the perpetrator and sometimes the victim. For those who believe, we must thank God that He has reserved a day for judgement, and the sinner will not go free (Ezekiel 18:4, 20; Rom 6:23; Rev 22:12). And, for those who realise the folly of their ways, and are genuinely remorseful of their horrific crimes against innocent men and women, and cry to God for forgiveness, we must thank God who forgives and cleanses sinners from all guilt. All sins are forgivable if we repent before God in humility and sincerity. We are told that only one sin is unpardonable, and that is blasphemy against the Holy Ghost.

#517 KNOWING JUST WHAT IS ENOUGH FOR US 34

We know just what is enough for us to know.

HOW do we answer the thorny questions in life? Why do good men die young? Why would a young girl be allowed to fall prey to a man who raped her? Why was a young Nigerian girl, Leah Sharibu, allowed to be captured by religious fundamentalists and detained against her will because she would not compromise her own religious beliefs? How do criminals manage to escape from justice? Why do children get cancers and some born disabled? What would a loving God allow the houses of poor peasants to be washed away by tsunamis, floods, mudslides, or destroyed by fire? Why would a hero be captured by enemy soldiers and tortured to death? Why are honest men booted out of their jobs, reduced to poverty, and forced to beg for a living whilst doing what was right? Why do dishonest men succeed and become wealthy on the back of hardworking, honest toilers? Why do serious diseases spare the bad men and strike the weak, poor, well-behaved amongst us?

The answers to these questions, if we are honest, are that we simply do not know. It boils down to the fact that we do not know how God does His things. Deuteronomy tells us,
"The secret things belong unto the Lord our God: but those things which are revealed belong unto us and to our children forever, that we may do all the words of this law" (Deut. 29:29).
There we have it – some things are secret, and God alone has the answers, but man must be content with what he needs to get by on earth. Some things that were "hidden" in the past have been revealed and explained by scientific discoveries. However, until the Lord returns, there are things that we will never be able to explain by human reasoning alone.

For His deep and unfathomable knowledge, we have reasons to praise the Lord.
534. Does not respect man
535. Does not see as man sees
536. Looks at the inward parts; at our motives, and our hearts
537. Knows our thoughts from afar off
538. Has a record of our sins but loves us all the same
539. Chooses to forget our iniquities
540. Has engraved our names on the palms of His hands (Isaiah 49:15)
541. Will write His name on our foreheads (Rev 22:4)
542. For the promise of eternal life in God's presence
543. He will never miscarry justice
544. Whatever He starts, He finishes

545. Forever, His word is settled in heaven
546. There is nothing too hard for the Lord; with Him, nothing is impossible
547. The earth is full of His goodness (Ps 119:64)
548. He answers prayers
549. He answers prayers in a way that favours us
550. In answering our prayers, He usually gives us what we need, not what we want.
551. He frequently gives us more than we ask for, or things we didn't think to ask.

#4 GOD LOVES ALL 35

Both God and His Son love us a great deal. However, this is love that some of us sometimes misunderstand or define wrongly. It is quite true that God loves ALL men. However, the Almighty, who is wholly righteous, cannot behold sin. He hates all sin. Thus, we know that God loves all men but hates all sin. It is possible to love men without loving or approving of the transgressions of God's laws. I would love my son, but if he steals from people and deprives them of their hard-earned resources, I must loathe his activities. Loving a man does not equate to approving their quirks, foibles, idiosyncrasies and habitual criminal acts. We must be loyal to our governments and their officials, but if such rule-bearers become detached, dictatorial or intolerant of peaceful and constructive criticism, then we do not have to like that regime. We will be harming the poor, weak and disadvantaged people in the population who will bear the brunt of a bad government's injudicious policy and the misery that bad decisions will heap upon them. However, the people of God are fortunate in that they are ruled and led by a just God who loves all men, hates sin, and is constantly looking for errant souls to return to sweet fellowship with Him.

GOD's CREATION

552. For creating man (Gen 1:27)
553. For giving us life and the breath of life (Gen 2:7)
554. For giving us a soul
555. For giving us our spirits
556. For giving our body which houses both the spirit and the soul
557. Making man the head of creation, putting him in charge (Gen 1:28)
558. The earth is the Lord's, and all the fulness thereof (Exodus 19:5, Ps 24:1)
559. For giving us mothers
560. Fathers
561. Brothers
562. Sisters
563. Other relatives who shape our lives
564. For blessing us and empowering us to increase and multiply
565. For our parents and their care for us
566. For giving us aunties, uncles, nieces, nephews and cousins.
567. For giving us children
568. For providing us with all the required resources for bringing up the children well
569. For our children who live away and the people who care for them
570. For our childhood friends and close confidants
571. For people who call (phone) us to ensure that we are well
572. For those who pray for us
573. For those who stand by us when we feel lonely.
574. For our teachers, pastors and mentors

575. For positioning us to be helpful to some work colleagues as mentors
576. Giving us company, making us social animals who live in communities (Gen 2:18)
577. Making us mutually dependent on one another
578. Creating helpers amongst us
579. Giving us social organization in government and workplaces
580. Providing us with the necessities of life such as free air to breathe
581. Giving us plants to use for food, medicine and furniture;
582. For the gift of Agriculture (and other arts, crafts and professions)
583. For creating animals
584. Fishes
585. Birds
586. Insects
587. Reptiles
588. For symbiotic bacteria such as Doderlin's bacilli that protect us
589. For bacteria that synthesize Vitamin B in our bowel (Klebsiella, E Coli, S Typhimurium)
590. For bacteria that clean up our biochemical wastes – such as oil spillage and refuse
591. For providing our gut with the *Intrinsic Factor,* which helps us to absorb Vitamin B_{12}
592. Weather, weather patterns and the changes in ambient temperature
593. Geographic features that beautify our world: landscapes, mountain ranges and seas.
594. For the immense power in volcanic eruptions
595. For the minerals released from volcanic ash that enrich soils for crops
596. For the power of hurricanes
597. For the ozone layer that protects us from the sun's ultraviolet radiation
598. Giving us water for our many uses (cooking, drinking, washing)
599. Water to wet our crops and farmlands

600. Oceans which produce 50% of the world's oxygen
601. Oceans which absorb most of the carbon dioxide we produce
602. Oceans which transport heat from the hot tropics to the colder poles,
603. Sea currents that bring warm air to the cold, and cold currents to cool the hot regions
604. For the food that the oceans produce – about 200 billion pounds per year
605. For the sea supply of table salt for seasoning and preservation of our food
606. For the recreation that the seas and oceans afford us
607. Oceans on which we can sail to move goods
608. And move people
609. For the Sun
610. For the moon and its effects on tides
611. For the stars in their beauty and their use for navigation
612. For our environmental weather.

257 FAITHFULNESS OF GOD – 1
The Night of Toil Note 36

The ways of God are beyond human understanding. It is easy to praise the Lord, as a song puts it, *"when the sun is shining down on me, when the world is all as it should be.14"*

It is easy to sing when we are rich, healthy and secure, and a steady flow of income is guaranteed. The test of our loyalty to God and of our faith is to keep thanking God when the world seems to be against

---

14 From "*Blessed be your name*" by Matt Reman, in *Musixmatch*.

us, we seem to be losing, and our effort appears not to be bearing fruit. Most people, Christians and non-Christians, have numerous examples of people who have faithfully toiled away under difficult circumstances.

An ancient book, *The Night of Toil, Or, a Familiar Account of the Labors of the First Missionaries in the South Sea Islands,*[15] edited by Favell Lee Mortimer and published just before 1894, described how thirty young missionaries set out on a ship, *The Duff,* from London on August 10 1796, to take Christianity to the island of Tahiti. Six were married with three children between them, and only four were ministers; the remaining fifteen were artisans in various trades. They arrived at Tahiti after a voyage of seven months on March 5, 1797. The English organisations that arranged, funded and sent the missionaries out were called *The Directors of the London Missionary Society*. The islands of the Pacific Ocean were called the South Sea Islands, of which Tahiti was the largest.

On arrival at the Pacific Islands, the natives met them with hostility, suspicion and difficulty. The missionaries had to contend with a language they did not understand, a culture that was alien and largely uncouth manners. Sydney in Australia, the nearest city that contained a smattering of British adventurists, was a few weeks away by boat. Sydney was called Jonestown in those days. In danger of tropical fevers and in danger of want; in danger of intertribal wars, in danger of theft of their irreplaceable belongings by the natives and in obvious peril that theirs was a journey of no-return, these servants of the Lord toiled away, trying to befriend the natives, giving practical aids to the natives, enduring, tolerating, persevering, praying, preaching, teaching, serving, loving and hoping. Coming back to England was out of the question: they were there to stay. Deprived of home comforts and sustained by their faith in the Lord, they soldiered on. It would take sixteen years before they made their

---

[15] *The Night of Toil, Or, A Familiar Account of the Labors of the First Missionaries in the South Sea Islands.* Editor: Favell Lee Mortimer. Circa 1894.

first converts – two men called Otio and Tuahine. Several years followed before the king accepted Christianity. They were faithful, and God was faithful, and Tahiti became a Christian nation.

Thirty-eight years after they set out from England in faith, this was recorded of them in the book:

"...*Their labor was not in vain in the Lord. In the end of the summer of 1835, many people in various parts of the island were converted, especially by the preaching of Mr. Nott at Papao.*"

Note: "**Many people** ... were converted ... by preaching" not by deception, coercion, force, manipulation, trickery or cheating but by pure love, just like Jesus, their master.

Today many Christian establishments fuss over temple size, crowd size, money, prosperity, miracles and wonders. But the great commission given by Jesus Christ to his followers before he went back to heaven was to "Go into all the world ...and make disciples of all nations, baptizing them ... (and) teaching them to observe all things that I have commanded you.[16]."

However, for people who obey the commission, who go on missionary assignments, who support missionary work in cash and in kind; who offer glasses of water to missionaries and evangelists in the name of the Lord, who take pity on the poor and all who endure hardship whilst remaining faithful to the call of God, we praise the Lord.

---

[16] Matthew 28:19-20; and Mark 16:15

257 THE FAITHFULNESS OF GOD – 2. note 37

The Svea Flood Story[17].

Pastor Cymbala wrote a beautiful story of God's faithfulness in an article titled *Unforeseen Fruit* which underlined Paul's reassurance to Timothy: "If we are faithless, God remains faithful because He cannot deny Himself." (2 Timothy 2:13.)

In 1921, a missionary couple called David and Svea Flood went from Sweden to Belgian Congo (later Zaire, and now Democratic Republic of Congo – DRC). They took along their two-year-old son. Already in Congo was another Scandinavian couple with whom they soon bonded. The Ericksons and the Floods set about evangelizing the natives.

However, the Chief of the village of N'dolera was hostile to the missionaries as he was protective of his traditional religion and did not want to upset his gods. The two couples were allowed to live outside the village. They erected their huts there. The only contact that the Chief allowed the missionaries was a young boy who would go to them to sell poultry and eggs. In time they witnessed to him, and he accepted the Lord Jesus Christ and became a born-again believer. Try as they might, there was no more fruit. Realizing their grim plight, the Ericksons went back to the central mission station, but the Floods persevered.

In time, Svea became pregnant. There was no hospital nearby and when she was about to give birth, the village Chief relented enough to allow a single midwife to assist her during labour. Being of small stature, her labour was difficult but she gave birth to a live baby girl.

---

[17] The Remarkable Story of Svea Flood – Pastor Jim Cymbala, accessed from https://cbnasia.org/home/2014/02. March 2020

The exhaustion, and possibly excessive blood loss caused puerperal illness from which she did not recover. About two and a half weeks after delivery, she succumbed and died, leaving behind baby Aina, her brother and her husband. Her husband buried her in a grave, marked it with a cross and, being completely disillusioned, decided to return to Sweden. He left the two children with missionaries at the mission station, saying, "God has ruined my life." He turned his back on God as he returned home.

The Ericksons themselves died of some tropical disease, and the two babies were passed over to some Americans in the mission. They changed Aina's name to "Aggie" and brought her with them to America when their stint ended three years later.

Aggie was raised in South Dakota and became a devoted and active Christian. She attended North Central Bible College in Minneapolis, where she met and married a Mr Dewy Hurst. The couple had two children. There was a significant Scandinavian presence amongst the people in the area. Several years later, she came across a Swedish religious magazine and inside it saw a photograph of a primitive location with a grave that had a white cross and an inscription "SVEA FLOOD." She found a translator who explained that "it was the story of a pair of missionaries who went to a village called N'dolera in 1921. The wife died after childbirth. A young African boy had been led to Christ and he built a school in the village and, in time, had won a lot of his students to Christ. The parents and the Chief had also become Christians."
Aggie sensed that the missionary must be her dad. She knew that her parents had given her to American missionaries to raise.

Excited, Aggie and her husband took a vacation to Sweden at the earliest opportunity and met her half-siblings. They warned her that her father was in bad shape, had begun to drink and lived alone. She found him in a dirty apartment, approached him, and they embraced.

The man was remorseful to her daughter, and they cried together. Aggie reassured him with her story, going to America, schooling, marriage and her children.

Her father interrupted her, "God ruined my life," he exclaimed.
"No, Papa," she reassured him. I have a little story to tell, and it is a true one. You did not go to Africa in vain, and Mama did not die in vain. Your only convert – the little boy that brought you food from the village – grew up and won the whole town to Christ. You planted just that one seed, but it kept growing and growing, and it yielded a hundred-fold fruit because today there are about six hundred Christian converts, including the village chief, serving the Lord because of your faithful ministry. God called you; you obeyed, went and prospered. Your labour was not in vain. See, God loves you and has never hated you.

They prayed together, and David re-committed his life to the Lord. Aggie and her husband went back to America after their holidays. A few weeks later, David Flood passed away – gone to be with his Maker.

A few years later, the Hursts attended a Christian conference in London, United Kingdom. They reported about the work of God in Zaire (the present-day Democratic Republic of the Congo). The country's superintendent of the national church spoke well of the impact and spread of the gospel in his nation and the 110,000 baptised believers. When Aggie went to chat with him, she asked if he had ever heard of David and Svea Flood. He answered in the affirmative that Svea Flood was the woman God used to lead him to Christ, that she was the most famous person in their history, and that he was the little boy that brought food to Aggie's parents. They embraced, hugged, and Aggie accepted an invitation to visit her mother's grave in the Congo. The trip happened and, whilst Aggie knelt to thank God for His faithfulness, the pastor read two passages from Scripture:

"I tell you the truth unless a grain of wheat falls into the ground and dies, it remains only a single seed. But if it dies, it produces many seeds[18]." Then he added:
"Those who sow in tears will reap in Joy[19]."

Somebody commented on this story thus:
"When you grow weary in the battle and think that what you do doesn't count, that you are a failure, remember the true story of David Flood and his wife, Svea. God promised, "My word...shall not return to Me void" (Isaiah 53:11, NKJV). The seed planted in the heart of one little boy resulted in a great harvest – one that David Flood couldn't see but one which God nurtured and brought to fruition.

"If we are faithless, yet God remains faithful: He cannot deny Himself" (2Tim 2:13 NKJV).
"Let us not become weary in doing good, for at the proper time we will reap a harvest if we do not give up." (Galatians 6:9 NIV).

613. Food, crops
614. Technological advances
615. And inventions
616. Medical discoveries
617. For bringing an end to wars like WW1, WW2, etc.
618. For governments and the administration of the nations

---

[18] John 12:24

[19] Psalm 126:5

619. For co-operation and fruitful alliances between nations
620. For religion and the freedom to choose one's faith
621. For the freedom to worship what one chooses
622. For missionaries that spread the word of God
623. For equipping teachers to explain the sacred texts
624. For giving the Bible as a compass to guide us to God
625. For the amazing way that Bible messages aligned – though written by several authors
626. Marriages
627. For the great things, God has done (Fanny Crosby) – giving His Son, Pardon and Love for us.
628. For the small things of life – they are great things that are so automatic to us that we hardly think of them[20]

626 APPRECIATING THE SMALL THINGS OF LIFE – 1 (The Thailand Moon) 38

Nelson Mandella, the great South African, said, *"It is only when one has been in prison that one appreciates the small things in life."*

---

[20] The GREAT LITTLE THINGS OF LIFE (#38) – (they come so automatically we hardly think of them)
Great little things or Little great things?

- *Blinking* - moistens the conjunctiva, which prevents eyes drying up
- *Yawning* – gives extra air intake
- *Swallowing* – an automatic reflex. It does not need to be taught.
- *Optical Reflex* – closing the eyes from incoming foreign bodies, blows and bright lights.
- *Tearing up* when any object touches our eye, the *Corneal Reflex* makes tears that wash dirt and harmful substances away. Dissolve bacteria by lysozyme enzymes and keeps the conjunctiva moist.
- *Scratching* – removes noxious stimuli.

What are the small things in life that we may not appreciate? How about seeing the Moon at night? Is that special? Here's how.

In 1998, a couple in my church informed me that an inmate of Thailand's notorious Bang Kwang prison tried to contact his relatives in Nigeria. He had gone to trade in jewellery but used the same hotels as some miscreants that the Thai police were following. When police stormed the hotel, they bolted, but he was arrested. He was asked to provide information about "his mates," but he denied knowing them – his misfortune was to check into the same hotel. Unable to prove his innocence or diffuse the police's suspicion, he was charged to court. Still protesting his innocence, he was thought to be impenitent and unremorseful and wrongly sent to jail. He was to serve life.

In prison, he became a Christian, and his attitude, humility and innocence made him win the hearts and sympathy of the American missionaries to the prison. They realized that he had been unable to contact his wife or family in the seven years he had spent. I joined a prayer group of six that was formed to pray for him. We started to correspond by mail and, in time, traced his mother and wife on one of my trips to Nigeria. The packages that my wife and I usually sent to him were paracetamol (for pains) and Nigerian periodicals – *Newswatch*, a Lagos monthly, and the newspapers *The Punch* or Nigeria *Sunday Times*.

It was about this time that he sent me a letter that contained *"an unusual request."* Unusual because he wrote, *"Brother Folorunso, please help me thank God that I saw the Moon tonight. Some of us were taken in a prison van to the hospital but we returned late after the last inmate had been seen by the doctors. On our Way back, the Moon was out and for the first time in seven years, I saw moonshine!"*

His reason for excitement and gratitude set me thinking. Here I am, seeing the Moon every day, **routinely**. So routine that I probably have never considered or regarded it as a privilege. In life, however, nothing, absolutely nothing, is routine. Imprisonment deprives the prisoner of his freedom." His sleeping and waking times, meal times and work schedule are dictated by total strangers, and he dares not object. How often have we needed to get out of bed on a work-free day, felt sleepy and lapsed back into bed for a little more lie-in? How often have we wanted to go and do some shopping or visit a friend but because we felt tired or the rain was drizzling we postponed the outing? How many times have we, on the spur of the moment, felt like having a cold drink from the refrigerator – and we went for it? These privileges are not available to inmates. Besides, you couldn't possibly postpone any routine in jail. Along this theme, we can thank God if we got soaked by the rain, saw a rainbow, had flies buzz in our ears as they were chasing and eating up decaying matter or helping us with pollinating crops.

"When two Englishmen meet, their first talk is of the weather," said poet Samuel Johnson. Weather-related comments in England include "This is a foul weather" (wet and windy), "I am freezing" (cold or wintry), "I am melting" (hot, in the summer) and "it is awful" (rainy and cloudy). Regardless of these, England always has sufficient water for its population. You might excuse the hyperboles, but there's a place in the Atacama Desert in Peru, South America, that is bone dry. As deserts go, this is the driest place on earth, and in some years, there is no rainfall. Like the Sahara in Africa, the days are roasting hot and the nights bone-numbing cold. For every single thing that we complain of having in excess, somewhere, someone is suffering from a lack of it: water, warm weather, food, visitors and work.

627 APPRECIATING THE SMALL THINGS OF LIFE – 2 (BREAKING WIND) 39

Would you thank God for breaking wind – malodorous wind?

In 2004, my university classmate who was one of my two best friends lay in the prestigious St Thomas's Hospital in London, dying. He had been flown in from Nigeria to receive the best medical care on offer because his family could afford the best for him. He told me that he had been eating in his home city of Owerri when he felt some strange pain in his lower jaw. A radiological examination revealed a fracture of his jaw bone. He was a senior doctor in his own right, having been elected as a Fellow of the Royal College of Obstetricians and Gynaecologists of London. The highest accolade for a Gynaecologist. He had a form of blood cancer that eats away at bones, renders them brittle and liable to fracture with minimal stress. Unfortunately, the cancer was advanced and had started to affect other parts of his body.

We first met at the university in Ibadan when we gained a *concessional* admission that allowed bright candidates to spend only one year in the university instead of the two that it took college pupils to achieve advanced level qualifications. At Ibadan, we felt drawn towards each other because we were both *born again Christians*. A few weeks into our preliminary (prelim) course, our friendship took off. We remained friends till 2004.

One of the worst social faux pas in our lives is to break wind in public. The wind we pass from our anus is usually smelly, antisocial, off-putting and bad etiquette. Sometimes, despite our most outstanding efforts to suppress it, it comes out with an explosive sound that is very embarrassing. It is one act that usually causes great embarrassment. If we passed wind, spouses and friends usually could tell that we were the culprit. They would equally feel our shame and might sometimes apologise on our behalf. Many people dishonestly deny being the culprit and instinctively try to shift the blame.

My friend was naturally gregarious and had a large circle of friends. His family was famous and very successful, and his extended family were just as massive. From amongst such company, when he became ill and was admitted into hospital, he appointed me as his spokesman and confidant. He chose me to be his public relations officer, updating his contacts on his progress or otherwise, and handling his prayer requests for supplications by his friends all over the world. In those days before *Facebook* or *Whatsapp*, electronic mail *(email)* was the primary means of rapid and mass dissemination of news to a closed circle of contacts. He would tell me what he wanted us to pray for, and I would announce it to our contacts.

One day, he gave me his latest prayer request: *"Help me thank God that I could break wind."*

In all my life, I had never known a man or woman deeming it fit to thank God for what embarrasses us; something we would rather not do in public, except in bathrooms, and for which we get embarrassed even if we were alone because the noise of its exit velocity sounds like a gun discharge. We usually cringe and go red-faced if a bathroom user in an adjacent cubicle hears our wind-breaking exploits or the futile attempts to suppress them because then, they come in salvos like the discharge of a semi-automatic gun.

My friend's bowels had stopped working, and he had been constipated for a few days. The bad thing about constipation is that it worsens over time. The primary function of our large bowel is to reabsorb water from our faeces and harden them; therefore, the longer it takes to empty our bowel, the more hard the motion becomes; the more chances that gases will build up from bacterial breakdown of matter within our bowels and the more discomfort we experience in opening our bowels. Such patients would have been given medications to stimulate the bowel muscles to contract and propel stool towards the exit. They might also be prescribed faecal softeners to help them get going.

Nurses might give an enema if the stool was hard and impacted in the lower end of the alimentary canal. For people who suffer from constipation, the first sign that relief is on its way is usually the passage of the gases that have built up with the faeces. As soon as there is a tiny opening around the stool, the gases fizzle out at jet-speed, but the smell would be redolent. On the night in question, my friend who had been constipated reached this stage, and he passed wind. As soon as that happened and before he passed any stool, he was thankful to God for that modicum of progress and wanted his friends to join him in thanking God, hence his unusual but understandable request for his praying partners to *join him thanking God that he could break wind.*

I ask you, who are reading this, have YOU ever thought that breaking wind is a compelling reason for you to thank God? I didn't – until that day. But now you know that every physiological action in the human body (*see page 66 below*), even if it appears odious and antisocial, like spitting, coughing up phlegm, blowing the nose, waking up with dried, crusted eye secretions, or ear wax, it is a reason to thank the Father of creation.

Here's a hymn written by someone who acknowledged God:

Immortal, invisible, God only wise,
In light inaccessible, hid from our eyes;
Most blessed, most glorious, the Ancient of Days,
Almighty, victorious, Thy great name we praise.

Unresting, unhasting, and silent as light,
Nor wanting, nor wasting, thou rulest in might;
Thy justice, like mountains, high soaring above,
Thy clouds which are fountains of goodness and love.

To all, life thou givest – to both great and small;
In all life thou livest, the true life of all;
We blossom and flourish as leaves on the tree,
And wither and perish – but naught changeth thee.

Great Father of glory, pure Father of light,
Thine angels adore thee, all veiling their sight;
All laud we would render: O help us to see
'Tis only the splendour of light hideth thee.

Walter C. Smith, 1876

Chapter 2 | **JESUS CHRIST**

LET'S TALK ABOUT JESUS!

Let's talk about Jesus,
Let all the world proclaim.
The pow'r and majesty
Of such a wondrous Name.
The Babe of Bethlehem,
The Bright and Morning Star,
Let's sing His praises near and far.

Let's talk about Jesus,
The Bread of Life is He,
The Saviour of the world,
The Man of Galilee.
The Prophet, Priest and King,
The Mighty God is He,
The well of Living Water free.

Let's talk about Jesus,
The Prince of Peace is He,
The Great Physician too,
Down through all history.
The Lily pure and white,
The Rose of Sharon fair,
The Shepherd of such tender care.

Let's talk about Jesus,
The Rock of Ages He,
The Lamb for sinners slain,
That Man of Calvary.
The Great Emmanuel,

115

The word of God sublime,
He is our Bridegroom so divine.

Let's talk about Jesus,
The King of Kings is He,
The Lord of lords supreme,
Through all eternity.
The Great I AM, the Way,
The Truth, the Life the Door,
Let's talk about Jesus more and more.

Herbert Buffum, (1879-1939)

HIS NAMES:

I thank you because

629. In Genesis, you are the Seed of the woman,
630. In Exodus, the Passover Lamb,
631. In Leviticus, the Lawgiver,
632. In Numbers, the Star out of Jacob,
633. In Deuteronomy, the Prophet, and
634. The Rock of our Salvation;
635. In Joshua, the Wall of our Defence;
636. In Ruth, you are the Loving Kinsman,
637. In Judges, the Righteous Judge,
638. In 1 Samuel, you are our Ebenezer, the Stone of Help, (7:12)
639. In 2 Samuel, the Light of Israel;
640. In 1 & 2 Kings, the Eternal King of Israel,
641. In 1 & 2 Chronicles, he is our Captain (2 Chr. 13:12)
642. In Ezra, the Holy Seed, (10:2)
643. In Nehemiah, the Joy of the Lord

644. In Esther, He is the Intercessor;
645. In Job, He is my Redeemer;
646. In Psalms, He is the King of Glory;
647. In Proverbs, the Fountain of all Wisdom,
648. In Ecclesiastes, The Creator;
649. In Songs, He is the Rose of Sharon, and
650. The Lily of the Valley.
651. In Isaiah, you are the prophesied child to be called Wonderful, (Isaiah 9:6)
652. The Counsellor,
653. The Mighty God,
654. The Everlasting Father,
655. The Prince of Peace (Is 9:6)
656. In Jeremiah, he is the Righteous Branch (Jer 23:5)
657. A King (ibid)
658. The Lord our Righteousness (Jer 23:6)
659. The Fountain of Living Waters;
660. The Balm of Gilead (8:22)
661. In Lamentations, he is the Joy of the whole earth (Lam 2:15),
662. In Ezekiel, he is the Plant of Renown,
663. In Daniel, he is the Messiah the Prince (Dan 9:25)
664. And the Son of God (Dan 3:25)
665. In Hosea and Joel, He is the Hope of His people (Joel 3:16);
666. In Amos and Obadiah, he is the Saviour coming to judge (Oba: 21)
667. In Jonah, he is the Messenger of God to men,
668. In Micah, he is the Judge of Israel,
669. In Nahum, he is the Stronghold in the day of trouble;
670. In Habakkuk, he is the Holy One,
671. In Zephaniah and Haggai, he is the Desire of Nations (Hag.2:7)
672. In Zechariah, he is the man whose name is The BRANCH (Zec. 3:8; 6:12)
673. The Soon-coming King (Zec. 14:9)
674. In Malachi, he is the Refiner and Purifier,
675. The Sun of Righteousness.
676. In Matthew, He is Emmanuel, Jesus who came to save us from our sins

677. The Master
678. The Great Physician,
679. The Friend of Sinners;
680. The Teacher.
681. In Mark, he is the Son of God
682. And the Son of Man
683. In Luke, he is Jesus of Nazareth
684. The Dayspring from on high, and,
685. The Son of the Highest;
686. In John, He is the Word
687. The Son of Man (12:23, 34)
688. The Light of the world, those that walk in Him shall not walk in darkness (8:12);[21]
689. The Bread of Life.
690. The Water of Life
691. The Door (10:7, 9)
692. The Good Shepherd (10:11)
693. The Resurrection and the Life (11:25)
694. The Lamb of God that takes away the sins of the world,
695. The Way,
696. The truth (14:6)
697. And the Life. (John 14:6)[22]

---

[21] **I am The Light of the world; he who follows me shall not walk in darkness, but shall have the light of life. (John 8:12).** *In the first instance, we thank our Creator for giving us the gift of sight. But the question that we need to ask is this, "Was Jesus Christ untruthful in his statements? Did he speak presumptuously or carelessly? Did he have any faults, especially with his assertions? Or, was he authoritative, truthful, credible and believable? If Christ was the holy, faultless being that the world acknowledges, then, his words must be true. He said emphatically, "I am the Light of the World." It follows that whoever does not walk in that light is in darkness. Without him, we cannot see where we are going. We will therefore grope, strain and argue blindly. We will stumble, hit obstacles and fall into small pits. We may trip up. We would certainly be genuine in our beliefs but genuinely wrong. Being genuinely wrong will not be an excuse before God Almighty. May God heal us from spiritual darkness and blindness!*

I was once guest at my brother's house in the Nigerian city of Abeokuta. I woke up in the night only to notice that the room was pitch dark because the electricity company had cut off supply to that neighbourhood as the available power was rationed. I stumbled out of bed in the direction of the bathroom. I couldn't see a thing, nor could I focus, tried as I might. I had arrived on holiday two nights previously, and my host – my younger brother Gboyega – had graciously run his electricity generator deep into the night. The noise would disturb the household, so generators are seldom left running all night long.

There was not even a scintilla of a light ray through the window behind my headboard. In pitch-black darkness, I fumbled for my torchlight. Not finding it easily, I lost patience because the urge to spend a penny was strong and I was mindful not to embarrass myself by suffering a urinary accident. I reverted to plan B – to feel my way out of trouble. I leaned against the bed, ran my hands along its edges and remembering the outlay of the room, groped to find the door between the bedroom and the *en suite* bathroom. Once through the door, I stuck my foot out gingerly and felt triumphant when I stubbed my big toe against the water closet.

At this stage, and just as I lifted up the lid of the water closet, the lights came on as power returned. The contrast was stark and incomparable. It was then I thought of what tragedy it is to be unsighted. And I thought of Christ's words that He is the Light of the world. Without him, we cannot see where we are going. We grope,

---

[22] Old school Song: *"I am the Way, the Truth and the Life,"* that's what Jesus said (2x). Without the Way, there is no going; Without the Truth, there is no knowing; Without the Life, there is no living. *"I am the Way, the Truth and The Life,"* That's what Jesus said.

we strain, we argue blindly. We stumble and hit obstacles and fall into pits, and may trip up. We miss our way and suffer minor and major accidents that the faintest of lights would have allowed us to anticipate and avoid. We would label things wrongly, or drink unclean fluids by wrongly thinking that they were wholesome. We would be genuine – but genuinely wrong.
May God heal us from spiritual blindness!

It is this type of difference that light makes to darkness that Christ was alluding to when he emphatically asserted that he was (and still is) the Light of the World. The sun gives us physical Light, but Jesus Christ gives us spiritual Light. 2000 years ago, he said, "I am the Light of the World, whoever follows me will not walk in darkness." (John 8:12). A man who walks in darkness cannot see where he is going nor can he perceive the dangers that lurk. He cannot appreciate if he might be walking into a ditch or stepping upon a serpent; he is at increased risk of falls, fractures, injuries, lacerations that might become infected and cause festering wounds or leg ulcers, not to speak of the inability to appreciate the beauty of nature. Spiritual blindness exposes us to being misled and deceived thereby becoming incognizant of what God likes or dislikes and we thus become easy prey to the Devil and lying ministers.

An old song said that "Without the way, there is no going; without the truth, there is no knowing and without the life, there is no living...." As Jesus Christ said that he is those things, it follows that a life without Jesus is a walk in the dark – a gamble fraught with falls; a life-walk that is off course and leads to a dead-end); a life devoid of the truth; a tragedy. When truth is absent, we embrace lies and deceptions, no matter how sugar-coated. By not knowing or having or living in truth, we lurch from deception to deception, from being tossed to and fro by those who themselves do not have the truth but profess to know it; and living a life that will come short when Jesus Christ comes to judge the world in righteousness. In the same passage where he asserted that he is the Way, Truth and Life (John 14), he said that he was going to die, go to heaven to prepare places for those who believe in him and that, he would one day come back to take us to himself. It is immaterial if we choose to disbelieve or even snigger: our belief or unbelief does not change the truth of the word of God or the assertion of Jesus Christ.

698. The True Vine (John 15:1)
699. In Acts, he is the Deliverer,
700. In 1 & 2 Corinthians, he is the Wisdom of God.
701. In Galatians, the Seed of Abraham,
702. In Ephesians, he is the Chief Cornerstone,
703. In Philippians, he is Jesus Christ,
704. In Colossians, he is the Head of the Church,
705. In 1 & 2 Thessalonians, he is 'The Lord Himself',
706. In 1 & 2 Timothy, he is the only Mediator between God and Man,[23]
707. In Titus, he is the Great God.
708. In Philemon, he is our Lord Jesus Christ,
709. In Hebrews, he is the Author and Finisher of our Faith
710. He is the same yesterday, today and forever (Heb 13:8)
711. In 1 & 2 Peter, he is the Shepherd
712. And Bishop of our Souls;
713. In 1 John, he is the Propitiation for our sins,
714. In 2 John, Son of the Father (v3)
715. In 3 John, he is our Fellow-helper to the truth.
716. In Jude, he is the Lord our Saviour; and,
717. In Revelations, he is the Alpha and the Omega (Rev 1:8, 11; 22:13);
718. The Beginning and the End, (22:13);

---

[23] For **there is one God and one Mediator between God and men, the Man Christ Jesus** who gave Himself a ransom for all ... I am speaking the truth in Christ and not lying. (1 Timothy 2:5-7, NKJV)

719. The First and the Last; (1:17, 22:13);
720. He who is, who was, and who is to come. (1:4, 8);
721. He who lived, and was dead and who is alive always (1:18);
722. The Almighty (1:8);
723. Amen (3:14); and,
724. He that has the keys of hell and death (1:18);
725. Jesus Christ (1:5)
726. The Faithful Witness (1:5)
727. The First-begotten of the dead (1:5)
728. The Prince of the kings of the earth (1:5)
729. He who loved us (1:5)
730. Him who has washed us from our sins in His blood (1:5)
731. He who has made us kings and priests to His God and his Father (1:6)
732. The Bright and Morning Star (22:16}
733. The faithful Witness (1:5)
734. The Word of God (1:2)
735. He who opens and no man shuts and shuts, and no man opens (3:7)
736. The Lion of the tribe of Judah (5:5)
737. The Root of David (5:5)
738. The Lamb (22:1,3)
739. Lord Jesus (22:20)
740. The Man of Calvary
741. The Prophet, Priest and King
742. And the Root and Offspring of David
743. The King of kings; and,
744. The Lord of Lords.

HIS DEEDS

745. Came into our world (his first coming)
746. Left all the glory of heaven behind to become a mortal man
747. Willingly left the glory of heaven for our sake
748. Loved us
749. Made himself low as to be born of a woman

750. For being born in a lowly manger
751. Followed the plan of salvation
752. Was obedient to God the Father
753. Dwelt amongst us
754. Revealed Himself to us.
755. Is touched with the feeling of our infirmities
756. Ever lives to make intercession for us before the throne of God.
757. Taught us facts by parables and direct references during his earthly ministry
758. Preached the Good News of God's love to us
759. Healed at the same time
760. Gave us the Sermon on the Mount
761. Showed us an example that we might follow in His steps
762. Taught us how to resist temptation
763. Taught us that Man shall not live by bread alone
764. Taught us not to lay up treasures where moth and rust corrupt (Mat 6:19)
765. Explained that we cannot serve God and Mammon
766. Taught us not to be anxious about tomorrow but to trust God for each day.
767. Taught us humility in the story of the praying Pharisee
768. Taught us self-examination in his handling of the woman caught in adultery
769. Taught us to rest
770. Taught us to pray
771. Taught us to evangelize and proselytize
772. Taught us to forgive
773. Taught us to be diligent
774. Taught us to fast
775. Taught us to pray
776. Taught us to teach
777. Taught us to preach
778. Taught us about marriage
779. For teaching us about divorce and remarriage
780. For teaching us not to swear
781. For teaching us to do to others what we expect them to do to us (Matt 7:12)

782. For teaching us to avoid hypocritical prayers
783. For teaching us to settle all disputes and unforgiveness before making offerings (Matt 5:23)
784. For teaching us to do almsgiving without drawing people's attention
785. For teaching us on money
786. Warned us not to make money our idol
787. Taught us not to worry about the future
788. Gave us the Lord's Prayer
789. Gave us parables
790. Showed us miracles
791. Taught us to refrain from anger (5:22)
792. Taught us to love our neighbour
793. Taught us how to be a good neighbour
794. Taught us to love our enemies
795. Taught us to bless those who curse us
796. Taught us to do good to those who use us despitefully and persecute us.
797. Taught us to avoid legal suits – "settle out of court!" Matt 5:25
798. Taught us to settle quarrels quickly, so we don't get dragged to courts (5:25)
799. Taught us that murder and adultery originate from the heart
800. Taught us to walk away from insults and maltreatment.
801. Taught us humility by washing the feet of his disciples: a servant's job!
802. Taught us not to discriminate based on race – by healing Romans and Samaritans.
803. Taught us not to practise racism or sexism – by conversing with a Samaritan woman by the well
804. Taught us not to be derogatory to the oppressed by touching lepers
805. Taught us not to be condescending to so-called criminals by eating with Zacchaeus
806. Taught us, in not castigating Peter when he lied, to take it easy with those who slip up;
807. Taught us, by addressing Thomas's doubts, to help those who ask obvious questions;

808. Taught us to seek the kingdom of God first, before earthly things
809. Taught us not to judge but to avoid wolves in our midst
810. Taught us to ask and to seek from God what we need
811. Warned us there would be tribulations
812. Reassured us He had overcome the world
813. Taught us to beware of false prophets and false Christs (Matt 7:15; Matt 24:4, Matt 24:11 and Matt 24:24).
814. Warned us that it is not everyone who calls Him 'Lord,' or prophesies, casts out devils, or does wonderful works or performs miracles that knows Christ, OR, is known by Christ (Matt 7:21-23). Some of them are workers of iniquity.
815. Taught us that, by their fruits, we shall identify false prophets
816. Taught us to be ready for His return
817. Taught us, by rising early to go to pray before work, the art of good preparation for each day.
818. Taught us the value of periodic separation and rest by saying, "Come ... and rest awhile."
819. Taught us with authority – not as a scribe (Matt.7:29)
820. Lived a sinless life, as an example to us
821. Receives sinful men – Simon the Leper, Nicodemus, you and I.
822. Heals lepers
823. Raises the dead
824. Makes blind eyes see
825. Makes the lame to walk again
826. Bears the iniquity of mankind
827. Instituted the Last Supper and invited us to dine at the table He has set for us.
828. Suffered for us that we might not suffer the wrath of God
829. Endured humiliation for us
830. Willingly laid down his life
831. He went to the cross where he was crucified
832. Made himself the sacrificial (Paschal) Lamb
833. Carried our sins on his person
834. Died for sinners.
835. Died for You and Me
836. Died that we might not die again

837. Bore his suffering on the cross stoically
838. We thank Jesus for His sacrificial death
839. Took captivity captive, defeating Hell and Death
840. Rose again on the third day
841. Triumphed over death in and the grave
842. Ascended into heaven
843. Opened the Way of salvation
844. Sent the Holy Spirit to us
845. Has gone up to prepare rooms for us (John 14:3)
846. He will come back to take us unto Himself (John 14:1-3)
847. Will gather us from all the four winds of the earth at his Second Coming.
848. Will keep us with him where he is, in glory.

AND WE THANK JESUS

849. For His parables
850. For His miracles
851. For his teachings
852. For coming to fulfil the Law
853. For teaching us to pray, and *how* to pray
854. For praying for us His followers
855. For teaching us to rest
856. For teaching us to prioritise our assignments (Story of "Lazarus is ill" & Mary/Martha – John 11)
857. For teaching us that all believers will be rewarded by the Father (Matt 20:1-16)
858. For instituting the Last Supper/Eucharist
859. For promising to come back at the end of the age
860. For His Second Coming
861. For continuing to heal the body, soul and mind
862. For making appearances to those people to whom He chooses to reveal Himself.

861 JESUS APPEARS TO PAKISTANI ARISTOCRAT #42

Mrs Bilquis Sheikh was the wife of a high-ranking minister in the Pakistani government. She was of noble birth and was influential and respected in her hometown near the border with Afghanistan. It was there that she had three mysterious encounters which changed her life and turned it down-upside from what she had ever known or imagined. She related her experiences in a book titled, *I dared to call him Father.*[24] She chose that title because her Muslim faith revers God so much that it did not permit adherents to call God "father." On the other hand, Christians are taught by Christ to pray and start with *"Our Father* who art in heaven...."

Bilquis had travelled the world, been to Mecca, and had a daughter who was a doctor in a city hospital. After separating from her husband, she took the grandson to live with her in the village where she had gone to settle. Her son became ill, and she searched for answers to many issues of life. She found a copy of the Bible and started browsing. She was curious that the Quran made many references to Jewish and Christian writings. That night, she had a dream.

In her dream, she was in the presence of a man that she knew must be Jesus. One minute, they sat at the table together; the next, she was on a mountain top and was able to name another man she saw in sandals: John the Baptist. When she woke up the next day, she knew nothing about John. Therefore, she yearned to read about him. Three days later, she had another dream. A man standing at her front door was selling perfumes, and she invited him in. He walked straight to her room, opened a vial of perfume, put it on the table beside her bed and as the fragrance permeated through the room, the man

---

[24] *I Dared to Call Him Father.* Bilquis Sheikh. Kingsway Publications. New Ed 2003

instructed her that the smell must go round the world. When she woke up the following day, she turned to where the perfume was placed in the dream but there was only one thing on the spot on the table: the Bible. Putting two and two together, she realized that the perfume, or Bible, must go round the world, or rather, that the message of the Bible must be spread far and wide. And she would be the vehicle by which the fragrance must be dispersed.

She did just that, facing stiff opposition in her village, derided, mocked, ostracized by her people who had once revered her, and she had to move away when certain people made threats to harm her physically and attempted to burn down her house. It was, however, the catalyst for her to flee her home country, but wherever she went, she took the gospel with her, spreading that fragrance.

Chapter 3 | THE HOLY SPIRIT

We praise God for:

863. The Holy Spirit, The Comforter (John 14:26; 16:7)
864. For giving Life (Gen 2:7; John 20:22; Eze. 37:8-10)
865. For creating Man (Psa. 104:30)
866. The Spirit blows the wind of life on believers (Job 4:15; Ez 37:8-10)
867. For bearing witness about Christ
868. For glorifying Christ (John 16:12-14)
869. For testifying of Christ (John 15:26)
870. For empowering the believer to testify of Christ to the world
871. For preparing us to enter the Kingdom of God (John 3:5)
872. For dwelling in us (1 Cor. 3:16; Rom 3:9)
873. Teaching us all truth (Rev. 2:7; Luke 12:12)
874. For bringing all things to our remembrance.
875. For guiding us into all truth (John 16:12-14)
876. Interceding for us at the throne of the Father (Rom. 8:26)
877. For baptizing us in and with the Holy Ghost.
878. The Giver of spiritual gifts
879. The power to speak in tongues
880. The knowledge to interpret tongues
881. Giving us Joy
882. Ministering to the needs of His saints
883. Speaking to us in the still small voice, in our dreams and Scripture
884. Walking with us along the narrow Way.
885. Bearing with us in our infirmity

886. Being a Comforter
887. For the work of the Holy Spirit amongst men – converting the soul
888. For being at work amongst believers
889. For giving believers unity
890. For being the Still, Small Voice that speaks to our conscience
891. For giving us the spiritual gifts of the Word of Wisdom,
892. Word of Knowledge,
893. Faith,
894. Gifts of Healings,
895. Working of Miracles,
896. Prophecy,
897. Distinguishing between spirits,
898. Tongues, and
899. Interpretation of Tongues
900. For making the church one body – and for making some of us
901. Apostles,
902. Prophets,
903. Evangelists,
904. Pastors, and,
905. Teachers
906. Also, for equipping some of us for Service
907. Ministry
908. Leadership,
909. Administration
910. Exhortation/encouragers
911. And making some of us Helpers, and
912. Giving us visions.
913. Thank you for giving us the gifts of celibacy,
914. Hospitality,
915. Ministry of Intercession

916. Ability to marry successfully, and move to marriage
917. Effective witnessing,
918. Ability to dream
919. Interpret dreams
920. Ability to have passion, visions and missions
921. And skill in secular professions of singing,
922. Composing music,
923. Poetry,
924. Writing
925. Oratory – preaching the Word of God,
926. Preparing the hearts of men to hear the word of God
927. To process what they hear
928. To understand the Truth about God and the gospel
929. To convict men of sin
930. Convincing them to come to the cross for forgiveness
931. Leading them to repentance
932. And pardoning our sins
933. Nurturing the young Christian
934. Helping to resist temptation
935. Encouraging and forgiving us if we should fail
936. Strengthens us (Eph 3:16)
937. Interceding for us before the Father
938. Leads and directs us (Matthew 4:1)
939. Speaks through us (Acts 1:4. 13:2, 28:25)
940. Gives us the power to cast out demons (Mat 12:28)
941. Anoints us (Acts 10:28)
942. Fills us (Acts 7:55)
943. Leads us into worship (John 4:23).
944. Dwells in us (1 Cor 3:16)
945. Gives health and strength
946. Guides us into all truth)

947. Shows us things to come) (John 16:13)
948. Releases prophesy, dreams and visions (Acts 10:19; 11:12)
949. Gives guidance (Acts 11:12)
950. Produces fruits in our lives (Gal 5:22; Psalm 92:14)
951. Helps us in our weakness (Rom 8:26)
952. Bears witness with our spirit that we are the children of God (Rom 8:16)
953. Bears witness of Christ (John5:32; 1 John 5:6)
954. Gives the power to mortify the works of the flesh (Rom 8:13)
955. Provides governance for witnessing and for preaching (Acts 1:8)
956. Searches the deep things of God (1 Cor. 2:10)
957. Quickens the mortal body (Rom 8:13)
958. Brings revelation (Luke 2:25; Eph 3:5)
959. Sanctifies and justifies us (Rom 15:16; 1 Tim 3:16)
960. He commissions us (Acts 13:4)
961. He convicts the world (John 16:8)

Chapter 4 | MAN-1: BODY IN HEALTH

962. For creating us
963. Creating male and female to complement one another
964. Giving humans the ability to reproduce after their kind
965. Blessing and commanding the first pair to multiply and replenish the earth
966. Clothing our nakedness
967. **I am wonderfully and fearfully made**
968. Waking me up each day
969. Helping my body to rest and be refreshed each night
970. The blessedness of siestas and catnaps
971. Allowing us to overcome sporadic insomnia
972. Giving us somewhere to lay our head each night – 'a roof over our head.'
973. Giving our body a biological clock
974. I was born complete: with fingers, toes and other organs.

#16 WONDERFULLY MADE – 2 Note #43 (see Note #1 page 12 for part 1)

We often see people that we cruelly label as monsters, freaks or medical oddities. We need to understand the complex events that occur during a baby's development in the womb to understand the things we occasionally see that do not conform to what is expected or, "*normal.*" For instance, we are all familiar with a set of identical twins. They are often beautiful to behold because of their stunning similarity and resemblance. They have to be because, at conception, they were one individual during the first week of life. Then "*something*" made them split into two individuals. When the split is perfect, we have two adorable babies. A slight delay in, or incompletion of, that splitting process causes imperfection that will be noticed as a variety of strange and rare medical conditions such as:

1. The division into two fetuses is incomplete, leading to conjoint twins. These are joined together at the pole opposite to where the division started. A developing baby has two poles – head and tail (caudal end). The head may be fused (when the division had started from the tail end), or the two babies may be joined together at the hips (when division has started at the head end).

2. The presence of conjoint twins explains why we might have individuals with two heads and three or four hands or feet. Sometimes, a pair may share a single internal organ like the heart or the liver. Understanding these might help us appreciate that these are not monsters but an accident during development that neither they nor their parents had control of. It is therefore cruel to attribute wrong-doing to such parents or the children. If you are not like them, and you are neither in their shoes nor their parents', you might never appreciate their heartache and their struggles. However, you need to thank God and perhaps develop some empathy.

3. *Fetus-in-fetu.*

   Sometimes, newspapers sensationally announce that a boy or a man is pregnant because a baby or a miscarriage had been found inside a man! Doctors might carry out surgery to remove the skeleton of a dead baby from inside the subject.

How did this happen?
In a normal pregnancy, the beginning of embryonic life sees a male and a female egg fuse together (**fertilization**). That occurs about 14 days after the beginning of a woman's menstrual period. The fused cell is called a *zygote*. This cell divides rapidly, and after about two weeks, now called an *embryo*, there is a flat sheet of cells. The sheet will fold itself, like a newspaper, into a tube by 28 days of conception with two ends – called *poles*.
In some cases (once in every 250 pregnancies), the single fertilized egg or *zygote* splits into two, and each half develops as a separate, distinct embryo resulting in a set of identical or *monozygotic* **twins**. That usually happens within the first week of conception. After nine months from the onset of menstruation, two distinct individuals will emerge as a set of identical twin babies.

Rarely, one embryo (sheet of cells) might inadvertently wrap itself around its twin during the folding process. The twin that wraps around its sibling will be born as a "normal" singleton baby. Usually, the twin inside its brother or sister (the parasitic twin) will continue to grow as long as it has an efficient blood supply bringing in nutrition. In some cases, it taps blood supply from the viable, enveloping twin and develops up to a stage that includes having a bony skeleton. As the host twin grows in size, it begins to squeeze the "imprisoned twin," cutting off all attachments to their mother. The parasite's size will thus be limited by the host twin's body inside which the parasite is trapped. Human features might develop, but at some stage, life and growth are no longer sustainable, and the parasite dies inside its sibling. It may become mummified. The flesh may disappear by digestion, but bones don't dissolve so readily.

Often, the host's abdomen will be distended by the presence of the parasitic twin. One or two arms or all four limbs may jut out of its host as flailing, lifeless appendages and any part of the parasite might be visible externally**. It is a parasite that the unfortunate host twin must carry about. Imaging procedures like X-rays or ultrasound scans allow doctors to visualize the extra skeletons of the parasitic twin. Those bones could be shown to the watching public as pregnancy within the surviving twin! The condition is called "*Fetus in fetu,*" or a baby inside another baby. It is sensational if the twins are male because of the medical curiosity having fetal bones inside them.

** (*See: Josephine Myrtle Corbin, The Four-legged Woman; b. 12 May 1868 in Tennessee USA. Died 6 May 1928. One body 4 legs*).

966 & 16 WONDERFULLY MADE – 3 note #44

Sometimes we meet people who are born with incomplete digits or members. Nine fingers, one hand missing or a foot or leg missing is not uncommon. In January 2021, the British Broadcasting Service aired the story of a young tennis player who was doing very well in her professional tennis career. She was missing a few fingers on one hand and one toe in a foot. Remarkably, she had adapted, accepted her condition without bitterness or complaints, and excelled in a niche where non-disabled peers were struggling to do well.

There are four possible embryological explanations:

1. Amniotic bands: Sometimes, tiny strings appear in the amniotic fluid that bathes a baby within the womb. These are called **amniotic bands,** and in some cases, the causes are obscure. Some cases have been associated with the procedure called **amniocentesis,** whereby a fine needle is inserted into the fluid to withdraw samples of it for prenatal diagnosis of specific disease conditions. Each band is a thin string made of protein

that is capable of constricting developing tissues. If a band or line wraps around a growing digit or limb, it could constrict its tiny blood supply and lead to the death of the body part – effectively a gradual amputation. It might not be cosmetically aesthetic to have nine toes or fingers, but as these individuals did not consciously choose to have fewer members, we should not bully or harass them; instead, we should thank God if all our members are complete.

2. Drugs: Certain medications taken by pregnant women may affect fetal development. These include anti-cancer drugs, certain anti-epileptics and thalidomide.

3. Exposure to radioactive substances can theoretically cause any part of the body of a growing fetus to not develop, such as in the babies born near the sites of two nuclear accidents in recent memory: Chernobyl, Russia in1986 and Fukushima, Japan, in 2011 in the wake of the tsunami.

4. Failure of the digit to develop due to a defect in the gene or the growth factor required in that particular area of the body. Some infections like meningitis may also cause us to lose limbs by causing tiny blood clots to block off oxygen delivery to our limbs.

975.   *I have the characteristics of a living organism*:

The following eight points are the functions that our body performs every day and distinguish us from inanimate objects or plants. They are called **the characteristics of a living thing**. It is easy for us to take these events as routine and non-providential. The mnemonic for a biology student to remember these is *MR NIGER DIES.*

976. I can **move** (**Movement**)[25]
977. I can breathe (**Respiration**)[26]:
978. I can eat (**Nutrition**)
979. I can feel sensation (**Irritability**)
980. I grow, my tissues grow (**Growth**)
981. I can excrete wastes (**Excretion**)
982. I can reproduce, or have the potential ability to do so; (**Reproduction**)
983. After our labour is done, each person **D**ies to go to rest permanently.
984. For muscles that move involuntarily but in a coordinated way (gut/bowel, heart)
985. For inbuilding into these muscles, the technical capacity to contract intrinsically.
986. I can do most, if not all, things in moderation**

---

[25] Movement is a complex process that involves several tissues and organs: The brain controls the nerves, which supply and stimulate the muscles that are attached to bones by tendons. The bones interlink at various joints that are held together by ligaments and muscles. Big joints are lubricated by synovial fluid. The ears and the eyes are also crucial in keeping the subject erect and preventing falls, missteps and unsteady gait.

[26] 2020 will go down in history as a year when breathing was the most talked-about physiological function. First was the difficulty that was experienced by the patients who suffered from advanced Covid-19 disease when plugs of mucus and inflammatory exudates clogged up the tiny airways (bronchioles) that convey oxygen to the airbags (alveoli) in the lungs. Secondly, "*I can't breathe*" was a phrase that became synonymous with protests against police handling of suspected criminals in the United States of America, in the wake of the death of Mr George Floyd in May.

986 ABILITY TO REGULATE ALL THINGS
(Homeostasis) *ho-mee-oh-stay-sees #45.*

Our body is programmed to regulate its activities within a narrow range of normal by an inbuilt mechanism that scientists call homeostasis. Every process in the body can be done to excess or inadequately. Sporadic coughs clear our throats of the debris that collect on its linings and help us get rid of bacteria that we inhale from the ambient air. Otherwise, they get into our lungs to cause infection or start cancer as asbestos does; however, if we cough too frequently, we irritate our neighbours.

If we cannot cough up at all because the phlegm is too thick, we have a problem – as people who suffer from cystic fibrosis experience. If we sweat normally, our sweat keeps our skin cool as the fluid evaporates; however, excessive sweating, *hyperhidrosis*, is unpleasant. At the other end of the spectrum are people who cannot sweat because of diseases such as *scleroderma*.

A normal appetite is good, but if you have an excessive urge to eat (polyphagia), you could become morbidly obese whereas, people with little or no appetite are anorexic and cachectic. For every condition and for each normal body function, there are some people on either side of "normal" who are below, or above 'the normal curve.' Examples include excessive urination (polyuria such as in diabetes) or too little urine (retention; oliguria), excessive height (gigantism) or dwarfed stature (cretinism); excessive joint mobility and limited movement of the joints; high blood pressure (hypertension) and very low blood pressure (hypotension); excessive activity of the thyroid gland (hyperthyroidism) and low activity of the gland (hypothyroidism). *Hyperthyroid* patients are on edge, anxious, sweaty, thin, have loose motions, eat a lot, have warm or hot body temperatures and are generally hyperactive. In contrast, *hypothyroid* patients are slow, sluggish, have poor appetite and tend to be overweight because their bodies burn energy slowly (slow metabolism). The best situation is to be *euthyroid* – to have just enough. Just like being euthyroid, the best place to be in life and in biology is bang in the middle of the population, in the group that statisticians call the *median mode* of a group of people.

Thus, if you have normal eyesight, hearing, height, body temperature, feelings, sleep, growth, walking gait, speech, and many such features, you have reasons to praise the Lord.

987. You allow me to enjoy youth before old age depreciation (death)
988. Giving me the grace to age gracefully
989. And to build up experience with age
990. Giving me a range of experiences to advise the youth with
991. Helping me to learn patience as I age
992. Allowing my age to earn me respect amongst youths
993. Saving me from certain death on numerous occasions
994. Death is not the end for me: children and memory live on
995. For the skeleton that supports me
996. For an intact neuromuscular system
997. For the endless supply of neuro-transmitters like acetyl-choline
998. For the speed of relay of impulses
999. I took my first **breath** at birth
1000. I can breathe
1001. My respiratory organs were formed and functional
1002. My trachea and bronchi are patent
1003. My air sacs opened quickly at birth (natural phospholipids)
1004. My vocal cords were formed and people heard me cry
1005. My epiglottis protects me from inhaling food particles
1006. Thanks for the mucus that keeps my respiratory passages moist and lubricated
1007. And for the cilia that waft particles up my throat
1008. Stabilizing my respiratory mucosa to be hypoallergenic (else, asthma!)

1009. Pneumocytes that allow gas exchange
1010. For the air I breathe – freely, abundantly and lavishly, (At altitude, the gas is thin) CO_2)
1011. Ability to draw in air and breathe same out – diaphragm, intercostal muscles working;
1012. Sealing my lungs in a protective cage of ribs
1013. Lubrication from the pleural, pericardiac and peritoneal fluids

1000 BREATHING EASY Note 46

2020 would be forever associated with the slogan "*I can't breathe.*" George Floyd, an American hip-hop artist, was in the process of being arrested by police. He had air surrounding him, good lungs and well-developed air passages as he lay dying, but he could not breathe. Another picture of 2020 was of a beautiful young Nigerian woman who was on admission for Covid-19-related complications. She held an oxygen mask to her face, but there seemed to be not enough gas, or whatever she was inhaling was not helping her effectively. She appeared forlorn and helpless. I hope she survived. Her air passages, and Mr Floyd's were mechanically obstructed.

A healthy man has plenty of air that he does not need to pay for. His air passages are usually open unless he suffers from an attack of asthma or he is being suffocated/strangulated. The air bags in the lungs where spent air (carbon dioxide) is exchanged for vital air (oxygen) are usually unimpeded unless there is water-logging inside or outside the lungs. Either of these will create the feeling of drowning. Fluid in the lungs happens in cases of pneumonia, heart failure, drowning, or viral storms. Fluid outside the exchange areas happens when the heart fails (pulmonary oedema, hydrothorax, bleeding into the chest, bacterial infections and lupus.) Sometimes we have no oxygen to breathe (at altitude; during carbon monoxide poisoning in an enclosed space or a carbon dioxide blanket during a volcanic eruption). All these are instances that make breathing difficult or impossible. Every day therefore that we are able to breathe easy calls for thanking God.

1014. I have mobility: bones support my frame
1015. Making my muscles supple[27] and responsive to nerve stimulation
1016. Attaching my muscles to bones and joints for smooth movements
1017. Regulating my gait such that I suffer no ataxia (loss of coordination)
1018. Giving me balance - body shape, skeleton, eyes, ears, cerebellum
1019. My bones are strong – not bent;
1020. Pain-free joint movement
1021. Joints that are not stiff
1022. Synovial fluid to lubricate my joints for smooth and pain-free movements
1023. Sufficient calcium and phosphate ions to build my bones
1024. Making cages for me to house and protect my pelvic organs
1025. As a woman, hiding my ovaries out of harm's way
1026. As a man, allowing my testicles to hang away from my body

---

[27] Some muscles are not supple at all. Some conditions can cause those muscles under our wilful control (*voluntary muscles*) to contract involuntarily and stay employed. One is *athetosis*, and another is tetanus infection when our mouths close and cannot be prised open (*lockjaw* or *trismus*, caused by *clostridium tetani* infection)

1027. Which preserves its reproductive function because it is cooler
1028. And prevents my developing testicular cancer
1029. In that position, guarding me against testicular torsion
1030. If torsion should happen, giving doctors skills to fix it (orchidopexy)
1031. Making a cage for my abdominal organs
1032. Giving me lungs, heart, liver and kidneys
1033. Giving me a skull that protects my brain from trauma
1034. The cerebrospinal fluid that cushions the effects of blows
1035. My skull protects my eyes and ears
1036. And my tongue is not bitten every time I talk or chew.
1037. Placing my eyes strategically to look forwards
1038. And my ears to the side
1039. Giving and helping me with memory
1040. Providing me with reflexes –
1041. The fetal Reflex for protection
1042. The sucking Reflex for Man and mammals
1043. Investing in me the instinct to not look directly at the sun
1044. Giving me the fright, flight or fight Reflex to preserve me from harm.
1045. And the hunger reflex to replenish my energy stores
1046. Having food to eat when I want to[28]
1047. Having a choice of menu whenever I desire to eat

---

[28] See the story *"Alive"* (See story #47)

(Reasons #61 p39 and #1046 p142)
GOD GIVES US OUR FOOD IN SEASON Story 47

*The eyes of all look to you, and **you give them their** food **at the** proper time. Ps 145:15*

Have you ever had food when you wanted it? Have you ever had to choose what you would eat from a set of a menu? Did you eat any warm food yesterday? Have you eaten at least three different types of food in the past seven days?
If you have answered "Yes" to any of those questions, then you might have reasons to praise the Lord.

A 15-man amateur Rugby team took off on a chartered plane from Montevideo in Uruguay for a match in Chile on the other side of the Andes. Five crew members, 25 friends and family, including five women, joined them aboard the military plane. The trip was expected to last for five days. The weather was terrible and forced an overnight stay in Mendoza, Argentina, at the foothills of the Andes, by the Chilean border. The next day, Friday the 13th of October 1972, the plane took off to conclude its journey. Poor visibility, strong winds and foul weather caused the plane to crash into a snow-filled ravine high up in the Andes. Rescue efforts did not locate them in the vast expanse of snowfields. The plane's roof was painted white and as that blended into the surroundings, it made sighting difficult. There were instant deaths and varying degrees of injuries, but some escaped without significant injury. Survivors could not make radio contact with rescue teams, and hope gradually faded after a few days. The plane's tail broke off with the original impact, but the fuselage was intact and provided shelter from the elements.

Realising that they had been given up for dead, they began to ration the little food available. When that food was exhausted, they shared the toothpaste found among the luggage. The little water available was what they could obtain by melting snow when the sun was shining. There was a lot of improvisation, and they had to contend with at least one deadly avalanche that took out two of them. Eventually, they completely ran out of food – any food.

It was at this stage that two of them, at the point of starving to death, did an unthinkable thing to keep them alive: they took tiny slices off one of the corpses that the icy conditions have preserved well. Gradually, all survivors joined in and partook in this survival fare but after several weeks, they began to run out of cadavers. It was only then that they came to the realisation that to stay up in the rarified environment with no prospect of sustenance or of rescue, was to merely delay the inevitable. Their only prospect was to find a way to come down the mountain to make contact with civilisation. The 17 who were still alive contributed warm clothing and food for two volunteers. They sent the duo away amidst tears that if they failed, they would all be doomed. The two gallant members would have to brave treacherous terrains, neck-deep snow, steep rock faces and several miles to seek help without a compass and with little hope. After ten days of arduous trek, they arrived at ground level and soon found villagers who were kind to usher them to the safety of a hut where they told tales of their incredible survival and of their friends still trapped high up in the mountains. Within two days, all 16 remaining survivors had been rescued. It had been 70 days since their plane crashed. Their story was carried by newspapers with the headline "ALIVE." That became the title of the book and the film that documented their story.

Of all the talking points in this story, perhaps the most touching and didactic is the thought that if we were sufficiently pushed to the wall, we would do things that we would not contemplate doing under normal circumstances. In extremis, we would eat food that we would normally disdain. The plane survivors had no food, had no choice of menu, had no warm food or hot drink and had to eat whatever was in their vicinity, at freezing temperatures *to keep body and soul together* – as long as it was edible.

For these reasons, if we have food and a choice of it, we ought always to praise the Lord.

*He **gives food** to every creature. His love endures forever.* (Ps 136:25)
*The eyes of all look to you, and you give them their **food** at the proper time/in due season.* (Ps 145:15)
All creatures look to you to provide them with their food at the appropriate time. (Ps 104:27)

1048. The ability to chew my food (mastication)
1049. Ability to swallow my food (deglutition)
1050. Ability to break down the complex food I eat (digestion)
1051. Ability to take the simple food into my tissues (absorption)
1052. Ability to make up complex substances from the simple food that I absorb (anabolism)
1053. Ability to break complex to simple food for energy use (catabolism)
1054. Ability to use food for energy (metabolism)
1055. The ability of my large bowel to store food remnants
1056. The power of my large bowel to reabsorb water from food contents
1057. Ability to look back and relish what I have just eaten[29]
1058. Blessing me with the satiety reflex - else I burst my stomach from overeating.

---

[29] It is said that the difference between a rich man and a poor man is that the rich man talks of his last meal, but the poor man thinks of his next meal. The former knows there would be a next meal while the other is concerned about where it will come from. If you can talk about your last meal, then, thank God.

1059. Putting acid in my stomach – to kill off most ingested bacteria
1060. And soften any bones that I eat
1061. Enzymes to digest my food
1062. Creating in me peristalsis to propel my food towards the large intestine
1063. Giving me absorptive surfaces (villi and intestinal folds)
1064. Bacteria in my terminal ileum to make Vitamin B_{12}
1065. Food moves along my gut without impedance.
1066. Providing various chemicals for my bodily functions:
1067. *Lysozymes* to digest unwanted tissues
1068. *Prostaglandins* to start labour and warn me of inflammation
1069. Phospholipids for lung maturity
1070. Cholesterol as the substrate for the synthesis of hormones
1071. Bile to digest fat
1072. Enzymes to break down food into absorbable units
1073. Hormones for various bodily functions
1074. Human Growth Hormone to help me grow normally
1075. But not excess of it, less I suffer from gigantism
1076. Sugar for cell metabolism;
1077. Sufficient insulin to regulate my blood sugar levels
1078. Or manufactured insulin that I can inject for the same purpose to control diabetes mellitus
1079. Angiotensin for blood pressure
1080. Catecholamines (adrenaline, noradrenaline) for blood pressure
1081. Prostacyclin for semen function
1082. Bathing my spermatozoa in life-giving prostatic fluid
1083. Tumour necrosis factor (TNF) to destroy early cancer
1084. And inflammatory chemicals to warn of potential danger.
1085. Enabling my body to synthesize vitamins D, B_{12} and oestrogen
1086. Creating fluid in my ear to maintain my balance
1087. Arranging the fluid in the semicircular canals to work in tandem with my brain
1088. Giving me eyes to supplement other structures to maintain balance
1089. Programming my body to produce MORE THAN THIRTY different types of fluids

1090. For the microorganisms on my body that prevent serious infections –
1091. For commensals and saprophytes (beneficial bacteria) that live in symbiosis, such as epidermal and vaginal flora and small intestinal bacteria that produce Vitamin B_{12}.

1084 BODY FLUIDS[30] 48

As you read this, there are over thirty different types of fluids that the human body makes. As we would expect, each of them has its function. The ones that quickly come to mind are blood, urine, sweat, tears and saliva. But most of our internal organs need to be bathed in or suspended in some fluids to protect them from external pressures by offering a cushioning effect to help eliminate waste products. For example, the brain is protected by the cushioning effect of *cerebrospinal fluid*[31] such that when we jerk our head or suffer a blow to the head as we take a tumble or bump into our wardrobes, we do not damage our brain. Some fluids are needed to keep delicate organs moist to prevent desiccation and chaffing, such as the eyes. People with a diseased condition that makes them produce no tears or less tear fluid than average tend to have frequent eye infections (conjunctivitis) and corneal ulcers. Dust particles, sand and pollen grains often come into our eyes on windy days or when we walk by

---

[30] They are at least 33 different types of fluids that the body produces. The more obvious ones are the blood, urine, tears, sweat, saliva, gastric juice, bile and milk.

[31] *Cerebrospinal fluid* =The central nervous system comprises the brain (*cerebrum*) and the spinal cord

the seashore, meadows or through the woods or dusty streets. These are washed down into our nasal cavities, and lysozyme enzymes in tear fluids kill off any bacteria in the impurity. From the nasal cavity, we can get rid of the build-up when we sneeze or blow our noses.

The semicircular fluid in our ears helps maintain our balance by informing our brain of our relative position (see *Keeping Our Balance, p23)*. Blood is the fluid of life. It carries food for the nutrition of our tissues, carries oxygen that is vital to giving us energy and returns carbon dioxide to the lungs, where it is traded for oxygen that is contained in the air that we inhale when we breathe. Furthermore, white cells in blood fight infections while platelets stop bleeding from cuts.

Blood keeps our body warm and, if the ambient temperature is high, it cools the body down by flowing to our extremities where dilated blood vessels lose heat. This is noticeable in dogs that pant with their tongues hanging out. Sweating also cools us down because as its water evaporates, it extracts the heat that is required to turn it into vapour from the body. Other important fluids help us digest or process food (saliva, gastric juice, bile, pancreatic juice); and provide food to nourish our newborn babies (milk, colostrum); Finally, two essential fluids are vital to the continuation of the human race by procreation: the follicular fluid in which a female egg (ovum) grows, and the seminal fluid which transports and nourishes male eggs (spermatozoa).

1092. **Respiration** – free air to breathe: no payment, no need for tubes or cylinders
1093. Keeping the air free from pollution as rain falls to remove particulate matter

1094. Saving us from suffocation[32]

1095. The expulsion of the waste products of metabolism (carbon dioxide)

1096. **NUTRITION** - availability of food,

1097. Knowledge of food-processing, cooking and food preparation

1098. Having appetite[33]

1099. Provision of our meals

1100. The hands that prepare our food

1101. Knowledge of farming

1102. The farmers that grow crops

1103. The hands that pick the fruits, mill the grains and transport the produce

1104. The cleanliness of our chefs and caterers (Typhoid Mary; Dirty chefs on TV)

1105. Preventing famine by filling our barns

---

[32] Suffocation can result from one of five reasons:
- Mechanical obstruction of the airways by external compression (strangulation);
- mechanical obstruction by internal blockage (choking) – food or tongue;
- reduction of the vagal system (Carotid body) as wrestlers do
- the mechanical compression of the rib cage and chest prevents lungs from expanding to take in oxygen by inspiration.
- Paralysis of the muscles of respiration like the diaphragm and intercostal muscles

These will cut off the external oxygen supply, prevent oxygen from reaching the tissues that exchange it for carbon dioxide and therefore, deprive the brain of oxygen.

[33] One cheeky prayer at mealtimes in my grammar school days goes thus:

Some have food but no appetite; some need but no food: For both food and desire, we thank thee, O Lord.

1106. Choice of food - ability or facility to say 'I don't want THAT food.'
1107. Ability to talk about our last meal
1108. Ability to smell the pleasing aroma of food
1109. The satisfaction of having a good dinner.
1110. Taste and taste buds
1111. Digestion
1112. Absorption
1113. Food storage in the liver and muscles
1114. Utilization (metabolism) of what is stored
1115. Giving us glucagon to mobilize glucose when required by our bodies
1116. Unobstructed passage of food and chyle into the intestines.
1117. **IRRITABILITY**: Touch. Our central nervous system
1118. Our five senses:
1119. I can see
1120. I can feel
1121. I can taste
1122. I can smell
1123. I can hear

1119 I CAN FEEL #49

Pain is unpleasant; however, the ability to feel the sensation of pain is a blessing to humanity. If our skin were numb, we would die in a matter of weeks from the injury that will not heal, from infections and a lack of blood supply.

One of my relatives told me that he looked at his foot one day and saw an ulcer. He could not tell for how long he had had the ulcer because he felt no pain. It prompted him to visit a doctor to check his blood sugar level as he suffered from adult-onset diabetes mellitus. His sugar was abnormally high, and within days, the foot was unsalvageable.[34].The diabetic condition had destroyed the nerves that allowed us to experience pain on those occasions when we step on painful objects or stub our toes. We would quickly withdraw them and care for any injury or breach of our skin. Failure to this might make bacteria to contaminate the wound and cause infections that can only spread. The diabetic foot is prone to have a reduced blood supply and neuropathy (nerve damage). Hence its wound does not heal in good time. If neglected or unspotted because it is not painful, it could cause us to have a discoloured, gangrenous foot due to insufficient blood supply *(ischaemia).* Another condition in which nerves are destroyed, causing loss of sensitivity and indifference to pain, is leprosy. The body's extremities – fingers, toes, ear lobes, and nose – therefore can be lost progressively as any injury to them is not appreciated. We do know that leprosy causes severe disfigurement.

1124. Ability to see near vision and long vision
1125. Ability to discern colour (no colour blindness)
1126. Ability to see clearly and sharply (no astigmatism)
1127. Sunlight to help us see by day
1128. Artificial light and the Moon to help us see at night
1129. Reflex to automatically shield our eyes from injury as missiles fly towards us
1130. Having the sense of hearing
1131. Having the sense of feeling – pain, heat, cold, sharp objects

---

[34] Half of all leg amputations are performed on people who have diabetes. The other 50% is due to trauma, infections (such as meningitis or tetanus) and cancer.

1132. Having the sense of taste
1133. Having the sense of smell
1134. **GROWTH** – that we grow day by day
1135. We grow physically
1136. We mature – acquiring knowledge and experience
1137. We grow in experience year on year
1138. We do not overgrow (gigantism)
1139. We do not undergrow (cretinism)
1140. Achieving developmental milestones (no precocious puberty, which embarrasses)
1141. Being unmolested by rapists, child molesters, abusive parents
1142. Reaching puberty normally
1143. Having a parent to confide in
1144. Discovering love; exhibiting affection; being loved
1145. Starting menstruation
1146. The structures that need to support us grow to meet our needs

1145 STARTING MENSTRUATION 51

Why starting menstruation is a reason to praise God.

In 1984, an English tabloid newspaper carried a sad story. In a secondary school class of 12 and 13-year-olds, one girl came into class one day, opened her locker and found a blood-stained lady's knicker. Intrigued, she wondered the reason behind the unusual "gift." Attached to the knicker was a note from one of the classmates that read, "YOU are the only girl in class who has not yet menstruated." When she arrived home that night, she hanged herself in her room. She had felt ashamed and out of place amongst her peers and felt that she was the abnormal, odd-woman-out. If she had had a close relationship with her mother or an older sister, she could have discussed the events at school with either, but she adjudged herself as a failure who was not fit to live.

How often young girls internalize their problems and act on misconceptions! How often a young person assumes that they are the worst beings alive when there are several millions who might be in worse positions? How often young adults expect themselves to be perfect when all that society and God expect of them is just to try their best – and their best is usually enough! If only people who feel depressed or disillusioned with life or circumstances around them will confide in a trusting adult such as a sibling, a parent, the class teacher, the general practitioner, the headteacher or the local priest!

There are many facets to this student's story.
First, achieving life's milestones matters to children as they grow up. They compare themselves to their peers. Both sexes discuss life matters among themselves and tease each other. That can sometimes lead to peer pressure.

Second, adolescents cannot weigh up the effects of their actions. The girl who taunted her mate could be described as cruel. However, she probably did not know that her relief and joy in starting her monthly periods could mean depression, humiliation, and suicidal thoughts for someone who is yet to reach that milestone in her young life.

Third, children of all ages need to have some rapport with their parents and be able to confide in them their feelings, fears, and struggles. Had this girl informed her mother of her ordeal, her mother would, in all probability, have reassured her that humans develop at different rates and somebody has to be the last to achieve a physiological landmark in any random group. Almost every girl menstruates by the age of 16. The few who might not would go to consult specialist Gynaecological Endocrinologist to investigate and manage the delayed menstruation. Some might even be menstruating, but the blood (menstruum) is not coming out of the body in the condition called *cryptomenorrhoea* or hidden menses.[35]

For this unfortunate girl, starting a regular menstrual cycle would have been a reason to praise God. Similar experiences might include conception, giving birth, starting to walk, starting to talk, going to school, owning a house, and so forth.

Biochemistry

1147. For all the biochemical reactions in my body each moment of the day
1148. Formation of enzymes (for example, absence of a particular enzyme causes albinism)
1149. Hormones (e.g., thyroxine and insulin – absence of these cause diabetes and goiter)
1150. Prostaglandins (mediate pain and initiation of labour)
1151. For adrenaline and noradrenaline, the fright fight or flight hormones; helps blood pressure.
1152. For cholesterol, the substrate for most steroid hormones

---

[35] Cryptomenorrhoea from Greek *cryptos* = hidden; *menos* = monthly periods. This happens when a membrane of tissue closes off the entrance into the vagina because, during fetal development, the said membrane does not disappear as it normally should do. Therefore, all the menstrual blood that had been lost builds up inside the vagina until a doctor incises it (usually in a cross-shaped fashion), and drains the blood.

1153. ATP - Adenosine Triphosphate (uses pyruvic and lactic acids which cause pain)
1154. Glycogen (Our body can store excess sugar as glycogen for when needed)
1155. Adipose tissue (we may complain of being fat, but absent body fat is *lipodystrophy*)
1156. No inborn errors of metabolism (some of us suffer from Phenyl Ketonuria, etc)

1157. **EXCRETION** – we are capable of excreting body wastes
1158. Giving our body homeostasis (self-regulation) to regulate salt and fluid balance
1159. The ability of the body to maintain core temperature regardless of the ambient temperature – thermoregulation[36]
1160. Setting up our biological rhythms – circadian, menstrual, cardiac, respiratory, sleep rhythms.
1161. We can pass wind through the mouth to prevent colic (like babies)[37]
1162. We can pass wind (flatus) to expel intestinal gas
1163. We 'can go' when we want to.
1164. The discovery of the Water Closet – previously, latrines were dug outside homes.
1165. We are continent of faeces.[38]

---

[36] Thermoregulation is how the brain maintains core body temperature at a reasonably constant narrow range, about 36.9°C. It keeps the vital (or central) organs – brain, lungs, heart, adrenals, kidneys and pancreas – perfused with blood despite the environmental [ambient] temperature. When it is very cold, our extremities – nose, ears, fingers, toes, even feet may become ischaemic and cold as blood is diverted away from them so that blood supply to the essential organs is maintained. The opposite, *Cooling,* was described earlier (Note #48, p84)

[37] When we pass wind from the mouth (belch, burp, eruct, flatulence), we are merely expelling gas that has built up in our stomach. We sometimes swallow gas from feeding greedily or having carbonated drinks. Our food also undergoes partial fermentation in our gut, producing gases.

1166. We can urinate (unlike in kidney failure *eclampsia* (pregnancy problem), when urine is reduced)
1167. We can pass urine in normal quantities[39]
1168. We are continent of urine URGE, STRESS, OVERFLOW AND FISTULA LEAKAGE are forms of incontinence,
1169. We do not have urinary retention (My first-ever patient had urinary retention; Relieved woman, 84 years)

REPRODUCTION

1170. Thank you for giving me distinct reproductive organs
1171. For making me capable of being a parent
1172. For making mankind reproduce after its kind
1173. For making each of us uniquely (such that we use face recognition, fingerprints, as ID)
1174. For making our eggs divide perfectly
1175. For achieving puberty
1176. For having secondary sex characteristics
1177. For the onset of menstruation
1178. For the miracle of conception
1179. For the definite formation of organs in-utero (embryology)
1180. For making ordinary cells develop into specialized tissues
1181. For starting the beating of the heart of every organism and man
1182. For fetal growth *in utero*

---

[38] Young women having their first babies but who have prolonged labours sometimes end up with faecal incontinence from damaged anal sphincters or even recto-vaginal fistula (a communication between the back and front passages). The elderly may have weak pelvic floor muscles and be incontinent of feces and urine.

[39] If we pass too much (polyuria), it could be diabetes. Too little volume (oliguria) could be dehydration or kidney disease; too frequently (frequency), it could be urinary tract infection or cystitis; if not frequently enough, it could be urinary retention. If we pass urine without problems, spare a thought for those who don't, and praise the Lord.

1183. For the natural and mysterious fluid that bathes a baby in the womb
1184. For the presence of this fluid that keeps babies beautiful, not squashed (otherwise they have Potter's facies)
1185. For creating a barrier in the placenta that shields a baby from harmful substances
1186. For pregnancy, wanted and unwanted
1187. For each baby conceived because you make all life
1188. For suffering no early pregnancy complications
1189. For those who suffer no miscarriage
1190. No cervical incompetence,
1191. No TORCH infection
1192. No amniotic bands
1193. No exposure to irradiation
1194. No abnormal placentation
1195. No placental Praevia and accreta[40]
1196. No pregnancy-induced hypertension
1197. No post-maturity
1198. For the spontaneous onset of labour and therefore, no need for induction[41]
1199. For preventing intra-uterine fetal deaths,
1200. For successful childbirth[42]

---

[40] The afterbirth (placenta) usually detaches from the womb after a baby is born. Occasionally (in about 1% of women), it is morbidly adherent to the womb wall and does not come off promptly, resulting in bleeding that could be fatal to the woman. Placenta are usually located above the upper two-thirds of the womb. In about 1% of women, the placenta is situated too low and close to the neck of the womb (cervix) where it infringes on the exit path of the baby. It could hold the head up and prevent normal delivery but more often, it tends to separate before the baby is born, causing bleeding (*haemorrhage*) before (*ante*) delivery (*partum*), that is, Antepartum haemorrhage, APH.

[41] Women usually go into labour spontaneously after 40 weeks of pregnancy, however, about a quarter of all pregnancies are now started or *induced* by the doctor or midwife,

[42] About 98% of deliveries result in the delivery of live babies. However, 1 in 200 women experience stillbirths.

1201. Avoiding the numerous complications of childbirth
1202. For a normal puerperium[43]
1203. Birth attendants,
1204. Good hospital facilities[44]
1205. Available pain killers
1206. Establishment of lactation
1207. No breast abscess
1208. Good bonding with baby
1209. Well enough to look after the baby – no Post-Partum Haemorrhage (PPH)
1210. No puerperal blues / post-natal depression (PND)
1211. No cause for Social Services to whisk the baby away
1212. Ventouse/Caesarean available to expedite delivery when necessary
1213. Uncomplicated operations[45]
1214. Visitors come to see the baby – health workers, community midwives, relatives
1215. For returning the female body to pre-pregnant status after delivery
1216. For the healing and return of the womb to normal

---

[43] The puerperium is the period of six weeks following delivery. Many women die from bleeding, infections, blood clots, or internal injuries sustained as the birth canal is torn or the womb is ruptured.

[44] It is easy to take maternity hospital facilities for granted. In the past, women went into labour at home, and many perish from hard labour. In S.W. Nigeria, up till a century ago, Yoruba women knelt to give birth; if the labour was difficult, they ended up with ulcers of the knees. That's now a thing of the past.

[45] Caesarean Section now accounts for 25% of deliveries in Britain. It is still a major operation and not to be taken lightly. Complications include anaesthetic problems, bleeding, damage to the bladder, blood clots, and death.

1170: CHILDLESSNESS (INFERTILITY) 52

Are you a parent? Have you ever been pregnant?

In Biblical times, a few famous women had a delay or total inability to become pregnant, such as Sarah, Rachel, Hannah and Manoah's wife. Sarah gave her maid to her husband to have a surrogate child; Rachel said to Jacob, *"Give me a child or I die."* She did – she died during labour for the delivery of Benjamin! Hannah was distraught, and her case was further aggravated by the taunts of Penninah, her husband's prolifically fecund first wife. Manoah's wife received prophetic words from the Angel of the Lord and gave birth to Samson (Judges 13).

Some women might never be pregnant, no matter how much they try. And there are men too, who are not equipped with the ability to become fathers. Approximately 1 in 8 (12%) of couples will not become parents naturally. The advent of assisted reproductive techniques (ART) has helped some couples, but that happens in well-resourced countries. Each ART cycle is expensive and sometimes, emotionally traumatic. It is not guaranteed to succeed. Where pregnancy is achieved, the miscarriage rate is high, and there is no certainty that an ART cycle – or several cycles – will result in the birth of a live baby. Each fertility clinic talks itself up in its success of achieving pregnancies. Pregnancy is half the story: what a prospective client should be asking is *'The take Home Baby Rate'* that is to say, of every hundred women who undergo an ART in a clinic, how many of them will take a live baby home? That is a tricky question. Doctors and Reproductive Medicine experts who assist women scientifically to get pregnant do not understand how a baby is made. That faculty belongs ONLY to God. The day that doctors understand how to cause a pregnancy, there will not be a single woman on earth who desires to have a baby but who cannot. The fact that we have infertile (barren, childless) women in our midst today testifies to man's poverty of the knowledge of how God gives babies to women.

From the foregoing, it is easy to see why any woman who gets pregnant ought to praise the Lord. In my career as a Gynaecologist, I have met women who, having been unable to achieve conception, crave for just a few weeks of pregnancy to experience early morning sickness and the feeling of a bulging tummy and tingly breasts. Those who get pregnant but habitually miscarry and therefore have no living children crave to experience the pangs of labour pains, the groaning accompanies the travail of labour, the feeling of a baby coming through the birth canal, the opportunity to give birth, and to cuddle a baby that is covered in meconium, amniotic fluid, and blood held tightly to their bodies. These *ordinary* experiences are the staple of women, even girls, who routinely give birth with metronomic regularity, sometimes at home, on farms, by the roadside, and in poorly equipped hospitals.

The causes of inability to have children (when tests have excluded the husband or partner as the likely culprit) include anatomical defects such as an absent birth canal; genetic defects such as Turner's or Noonan's syndrome; the absence of female eggs; inability to shed eggs (anovulation such as in Polycystic Ovarian Syndrome, PCO), or recurrent (habitual) miscarriage. In some instances, the woman gets pregnant but typically miscarries in the second trimester of pregnancy because the neck of the womb, the cervix, is somewhat loose (incompetent). Others lose full-term pregnancies repeatedly because of a condition in which antibodies destroy the baby's blood and render them severely anaemic or even "bloodless." That is caused by Rhesus incompatibility and is treatable by giving injections that neutralize the antibodies.

Male partners of women who cannot achieve pregnancy usually have problems with their eggs (spermatozoa). In rare cases, the male egg is absent entirely due to an error in brain function; or, eggs are formed, but they are too few in number, or a significant number of them are abnormal. Man does not yet know, in A.D. 2021, why a man needs to ejaculate up to 500 million male eggs in a single act of intercourse for just one of them to fertilise his wife's egg.[46] These are mysteries that reproductive science will need to elucidate in the future, if it can.

Sometimes, a man has eggs, but their route out of the body is blocked in the tube that conducts them (*the vas deferens* – the tube that is snipped during a *vas*-ectomy surgery).

It is when all these factors in a woman and her sexual partner are right and optimum, that a baby can be conceived (fertilisation). After conception comes the growth of the baby in the womb (gestation). Next is the process of delivering the baby (parturition). Any significant disturbance of these processes will result in no baby at all, and then, they have to try again. Meanwhile, *the biological clock of the woman* is ticking away. Each woman has a window of about 30-40 years to get pregnant and have her babies – about 14 to 50 years. It gets difficult once a woman advances beyond 40.

Finally, many babies perish during childbirth or shortly afterwards. Some die in infancy or childhood, and there are women who are unable to have more than one child. If such a child dies, the woman would be regarded as "childless!"

In light of these, each baby born to us, and raised to adolescence, calls for praises to God. Each life is precious, but it is only God who makes all these processes possible seamlessly.

---

[46] During an act of intercourse, a man ejaculates 2 - 8 millilitres (average 5ml or a teaspoonful) of semen at the first go. The number of spermatozoa in each millilitre is about 40-100 million. If we took 50 million as average, then a 5ml of semen would contain 250 million eggs. Most men would ejaculate again, about 30-60 minutes after the first act, although the density of sperm decreases with repeated ejaculation in the same session. Hence, a woman is inoculated with about 200 million to 1 billion eggs at a session of intercourse. Of these, **ONLY ONE** is needed to fertilise a female egg. We know that every woman does not get pregnant with just one act of coitus – sometimes, not even in her lifetime, as happens with women who couldn't conceive. Why do we need so many eggs to achieve a single pregnancy? Answer: **we don't know**! But God does. Therefore, if you have ever been pregnant, regardless of the outcome, it is time to praise the Lord!

1217. For the blessing of **miscarriage** (see story #53)
1218. The heartache that miscarriage prevents* (see #53)
1219. The ability to conceive again after a miscarriage
1220. For allowing certain pregnancies to continue generally after threatening to abort
1221. Forgiving the strength and optimism to try to conceive again after a miscarriage
1222. For the natural processes that clean up the womb cavity after a miscarriage
1223. For the natural processes that minimise blood loss following a miscarriage.

1216 WHAT BLESSING CAN THERE BE IN A MISCARRIAGE? (#53)

A miscarriage is often a painful, heart-wrenching and sad event. Some women might even miscarry several pregnancies in succession. Some women miscarry babies that have been conceived after considerable financial and emotional outlays on assisted conception procedures like *in vitro fertilization* (IVF). After miscarriages, some women try but fail to ever to conceive again. Miscarriages are very painful physically because the fetus and placenta, no matter how small, stretch the neck of the womb very painfully. This is usually accompanied by considerable blood loss. The dilatation of the cervix may cause fainting but more commonly, a woman may lose considerable blood that may threaten, or take life. In certain countries, bacterial infection may follow and cause disability or death.

So why will a miscarriage be a blessing?

It is rare for normally-formed fetuses to be miscarried. Although gynaecologists still do not know all the causes of miscarriage, especially where the fetus appears to have no abnormality, it is known that about half (51%) of miscarriages are due to abnormalities in the fetus, especially its chromosomal composition. Chromosomes are the genes that a baby inherits from its father and its mother at fertilisation, and they carry the adult characteristics of the parents. Ideally, each baby receives 23 chromosomes from each parent to form an adult complement of 46. Any slight deviation from this exact figure usually results in a miscarriage or, worse, disability in the child. The common conditions that we might encounter where a baby might be born with inexact number of chromosomes are Down's syndrome, Turner's Syndrome, Noonan's Syndrome and Klinefelter's Syndrome. There are rarer ones. One non-chromosomal condition is Androgen Insensitivity Syndrome (AIS, formerly called Testicular Feminisation Syndrome).

In Down's syndrome[47], the baby has an extra chromosome on pair number 21 (All 46 chromosomes are usually paired up from the largest – pair number 1 – to the smallest, pair number 22. The 23rd pair are the sex chromosomes, x, and y). This presence of the extra chromosome produces a baby who has a few features that may upset the parents: certain facial features, a tongue that appears big for the mouth, and some internal abnormalities such as 'a hole in the heart' (septal defects). The babies are playful and lovable, but they need extra care than the "ordinary" child. Childhood developmental milestones may lag behind those of children who have a full complement of chromosomes.

In two other syndromes, the extra chromosome appears on pair number 13 (Patau Syndrome) and 18 (Edwards' Syndrome). Although generally incompatible with life, about ten of such babies exist worldwide, with considerable disabilities.

---

[47] The presence of three chromosomes on pair number 21 gives its other name: Trisomy 21

The "opposite" of Down's Syndrome is Turner's whereby a baby has one fewer chromosomes that 46. The baby is always a female and her chromosomal complement is 44xo. (The normal is 44xy; the 0 in Turner's denotes the absence of a chromosome). These girls survive to early adulthood, they are often short-statured (less than 5 feet tall), have a webbed neck, and, amongst many other features, are unable to become mothers because they do not have functional ovaries or fully developed wombs.

In AIS, a baby who was conceived as a boy has testicles which cannot produce the male hormone, androgen. Or if produced, the tissues that ought to develop along male lines refuse to do so because they are insensitive to the androgen available. Such babies will therefore develop and grow up as females. There is no vagina (but there are no testicles in the scrotum either – they are often held up in the groin during their migration from the abdomen in the first few months of fetal development. The girl will grow up with the characteristics of a female child: smooth voice, well-developed breast, a female body, contour, long hairs, and so on, BUT the first hint of trouble is that she will not menstruate when her peers reach puberty and menarche. The absence of a menstrual period is what usually brings her into contact with a Gynaecologist.

Most of these abnormalities are detected by our bodies and majority of such pregnancies are aborted spontaneously by women. Up to three quarters will be miscarried in the first eight weeks of a pregnancy and a few more by the thirteenth week (the end of the first trimester of pregnancy.) In some rare cases, a miscarriage can still occur up to 24 weeks, after which a fetus legally becomes a baby. Medically speaking, a baby is capable of being born alive from 22 weeks onwards. A woman who is desperate to keep her pregnancy may prevail upon a doctor to offer hormones, womb relaxants, blood thinning agents or an operation to tighten the neck of a womb that is dilating in bid to keep the fetus in the womb. However, in a significant number of cases, it might be counter- productive to interfere with natural processes. As a rule of the thumb, normal pregnancies tend to progress to maturity; abnormal ones tend to be miscarried for one reason or the other. From the foregoing, a miscarriage might be God's and the body's ploy to rid the body of a fetus that has not been perfectly formed, rather than be saddled with a baby that will need enormous care and resources throughout its lifetime. When nature tries to be kind to us, we just might be focusing on the short term without realising that several years of struggle lie ahead.

Today, gynaecological science does not intervene in the first trimester if a pregnancy is showing signs of miscarrying (threatened miscarriage). A deeper discussion of this subject is beyond the scope of this short book, but suffice it to say that if and when we miscarry, we may thank God who might have stopped a pregnancy whose outcome we might not be entirely happy with six or seven months down the line.

DEATH & DYING

1224. Peaceful deaths
1225. Deaths that give eternal rest
1226. Deaths that end suffering
1227. Deaths that were sacrificial for a noble cause[48]
1228. Grace to plan for it (For those who have the grace to prepare their deaths)
1229. Time, legal competence, and grace to make a will
1230. To be survived by children
1231. To leave a good legacy
1232. The opportunity to say final "farewells."

---

[48] Many people have died to achieve freedom for others, Jesus Christ, Stephen, and Mothers who are diagnosed with cancer during pregnancy yet bravely carry on till their babies have a chance of survival with the full knowledge that each day's delay reduces their own chances of survival.

1233. The special grace that some people have to receive salvation near the time of death
1234. The providence to be surrounded by loved ones on death beds
1235. Quick, painless deaths without suffering
1236. Slow deaths that allow one to put their house in order
1237. The comfort that God gives to bereaved people
1238. The promise to never leave them alone nor forsake them
1239. The knowledge that those who die in the Lord go to rest in His bosom
1240. The hope of resurrection with the Lord
1241. The promise of eternal life with God

GENERAL HEALTH

1242. Being blessed with good health
1243. The availability of doctors, nurses, and allied health workers
1244. The knowledge and skill of doctors
1245. Doctors making the right decisions when treating us
1246. Doctors, nurses, and midwives who work out of hours and through the nights
1247. Successful outcomes of treatments
1248. The successful conduct of surgical procedures
1249. The role of Anaesthetists
1250. Successful intubations and inserting of spinal/epidural needles
1251. Patients waking up after anaesthesia
1252. Accident and Emergency departments
1253. Availability of drugs to treat ailments
1254. The availability of blood transfusion amenities

1255. Regulatory bodies which ensure the safety of medicines and ethical practice
1256. Safety of medications; lack of debilitating side effects
1257. Knowledge of herbal remedies in the local environment
1258. Health-giving leaves (tea, coca), herbs (coffee) for man
1259. Life-saving fungi producing ergometrine and synthetic derivatives of ergot
1260. Serendipitous discoveries of cures like ascorbic acid for scurvy
1261. Researched discoveries like vaccinations
1262. Medical pioneers like Jenner, Pasteur, Koch
1263. Knowledge of diseases and vectors and control of disease
1264. The provision of health care facilities by governments
1265. The British National Health Service, or each country's health services
1266. The Welfare state and assistance to low-income families
1267. Carers in the community or amongst relatives
1268. Availability of emergency services like Fire and Ambulance, Lifeboats, Police
1269. Provision of Care for the Elderly and vulnerable individuals
1270. Kind-hearted people looking after people with disability
1271. For the lessons that ill-health teaches us:
1272. Especially allowing the world to experience Covid-19 in 2020 when we all realised that:
1273. We do not need too many clothes
1274. We do not need too many shoes
1275. We do not always need all the food in our refrigerators
1276. We do not need too much food
1277. We need to interact socially for good mental health
1278. We can perform some of the work we rush to do in the office from home
1279. Some professions that we disdain such as Wastes and Refuse disposal are crucial
1280. Some work that we spend time on, like entertainment, are not essential as food
1281. It is only by the mercy of God that we are not consumed
1282. God's mercies are new every day

1283. We are happier when we have friends to share in our good fortunes
1284. It is truly not good for man to be alone: we need helpers and helpmates
1285. We depend on many people for our survival, Thus
1286. Thank you for our food producers
1287. Thank you for our food processors
1288. Thank you for our food transporters
1289. Thank you for environmental sanitation
1290. Thank you to environmental health officers that ensure the safety of our food
1291. Thank you for sanitation officers who keep our streets clean
1292. Thank you for the pasteurization of our milk
1293. Thank you for our supermarket shelf stockers
1294. Thank you for the cash-till operator and the bank teller
1295. Thank you for the availability of food and essential supply in our stores
1296. Thank you for the ability to visit food shops
1297. Thank you for the ability to choose and buy what we want or need
1298. Thank you for giving us a variety of foodstuff to choose from when shopping
1299. Thank you for regulatory bodies for the safety of medicines
1300. Thank you for factories that manufacture our drugs and vaccines
1301. Thank you for the availability of vaccines to those who need them
1302. Thank you for the ability of vaccines to protect us against infectious diseases
1303. Thank you for preventing common infections from overcoming us
1304. Thank you for the pandemics that happened in the past: they did not last long enough to wipe man off the face of the earth, but they made us think of You
1305. Thank you for our immune response to vaccinations as we produce antibodies

1306. Thank you for our immune response to, and ability to fight off infections
1307. Thank you for helping us to become immune to certain diseases like Small Pox and polio
1308. Thank you for making certain parts of the world too hot or too cold for some viruses
1309. Thank you for making youths relatively immune to illnesses: they are the workforce
1310. Thank you for those who risk their safety to make people well (see Health workers)
1311. Thank you for teaching the world the principles of controlling infectious diseases long before we discovered what germs were
1312. Thank you for the principles of disease prevention by 'hands, face and space.' [49]
1313. That isolation of infected individuals and washing of those who come into contact with them is advisable – even commanded by God. (Numbers 19)

1311 HANDS, FACE, AND SPACE IN THE BIBLE – Bible's "Covid" #54

Interestingly, but not surprising, the concept of isolating an infectious individual from the broader society as a preventive action to safeguard public health started in the Bible.

---

[49] The concept of quarantine after contact with infectious diseases and washing ourselves to be rid of pathogens was first mentioned in Leviticus 13:4 &46; Lev 14:8

In giving the Mosaic Laws to the children of Israel, God expressly instructed Moses to inform the children of Israel that, when any person died from an infectious or suppurative disease, the corpse must be carried outside the camp. The people who touched the corpse would be ceremonially unclean and could not rejoin the body of the people until they had washed themselves in the evening. If the dead person had a weeping sore, those who came into contact with him must isolate themselves from the congregation for SEVEN days, wash, and might then rejoin. The house in which a leper lived (leprosy was the term given to a wide variety of skin infections) must be washed and scrubbed with hyssop and cedar. (Numbers 5:1-4; Numbers 19). Now, biochemical analysis has shown that hyssop and cedar contain anti-bacterial, anti-viral and anti-fungal chemicals. In all these cases, God DID NOT EXPLAIN the minutiae of why He gave the Laws – He just wanted them to be believed and obeyed, nothing questioning. If anybody had wanted to know the reasons, the answer would have been, "We don't know." Cynics, atheists and apostates would have mocked that it was mindless obedience to an irrational law. During biblical times, nobody knew about microbes.

It took another 4,500 years before a raft of scientists, one after the other in the space of fifty years from 1820 to 1870, discovered unseen particles that they called, firstly *animalcule* and later, bacteria. The term *virus* would come later. Before men like Ignaz Semmelweis, Robert Koch, and Louis Pasteur discovered these "germs" under the microscope, doctors examined women who had given birth bare hands, performed surgery with bare, ungloved hands and initially denied that there were tiny germs on their hands that they were unwittingly transmitting to women. When Alexander Fleming discovered Penicillin, the outlook for infected persons improved dramatically. Until then, the best protection was PREVENTION: washing (HANDS) and isolation (SPACE). '*Hands, Face and Space*' was the slogan adopted by the British government during the worldwide coronavirus pandemic of 2020-2021, a debilitating and economically destructive viral pestilence that caused the COVID-19 illness.

But God saw all of man's struggles in the time of Moses. He knew that careful prevention would reduce infectivity, debility and fatality. He prescribed isolation and washing. The people could not see what they needed to wash. Or why. However, those who believed were the wise ones. The supposedly wise ones who scoffed at this advice were the foolish ones.

Sadly, this exact scenario will play out one more time in the future: God has commanded that we all need to be born again and be washed in Jesus Christ's blood in order to be clean. Some of us have mocked. Some laugh in derision. One recent American president said that he did not need to repent or be washed of any stain. If that was true, he is like some of us, who see no need for Christ or Christ's remedy for sin. Such people think that they know more than God. So did the doctors until the day of Dr. Ignaz Semmelweis. His intervention saved millions of women from death from *Childbed fever (Streptococcal Endometritis)*. We have another chance to obey a modern-day Mosaic Law to "Wash, and be clean." The choice is ours. However, for those who have been washed in the blood of the Lamb, praise be. For the teaching of isolation of infective patients, glory be. For our microbiologists, the distinction is unto God. For our microbiologists and virologists, praise be unto God. For giving us examples of public health practice in ancient times, we praise the Lord.

1314. For helping our body to fight **CANCER**-causing organisms
1315. Forgiving us Killer cells and Interferons that fight early cancer
1316. For allowing precancerous stages when such cells can be
        detected and treated
1317. For cancer specialists and the research they do

1318. For those whose bodies overcome cancers even at advanced stages
1319. For the care that people living with advanced cancer receive, especially in hospices
1320. For the grace to endure late cancer pains
1321. For **governments** and political systems
1322. **Government** provision of State Pensions and other benefits
1323. For systems of governments and social setups
1324. Free voting rights to elect our leaders
1325. For all leaders and heads of state, kings, queens, princes
1326. All other people in authority (Executives and ministers)
1327. Those who advise them – in politics, finance, and security
1328. For demography and its uses in planning and care
1329. For fundamental human rights
1330. For those who fought for fundamental human rights
1331. For freedom from slavery, oppression, dictatorship, and exploitation
1332. For the privilege and freedom of religious worship
1333. For the freedom to exist without the fear of being enslaved
1334. Absence of wars;
1335. For people who carry out mediation in, and cessation of conflicts
1336. For allowing past wars to cease
1337. And rehabilitating victims of war
1338. For the custodians of security – military, police, other law enforcement officers
1339. Decision-makers/parliamentarians, legislators
1340. The judiciary, Law and Order that separates us from animals
1341. Captains of industry
1342. Manufacturers
1343. Traders, commerce, industry and manufacture
1344. Other employees in essential services, artisans, and those who entertain
1345. For Trade and Commerce, Industry, Manufacturing and Processing
1346. For free-market enterprises
1347. For the availability of goods that are exchanged,

1348. For the suppliers of raw materials; farmers, planters, harvesters, transporters
1349. For processing plants and the skill to transport perishables
1350. For guiding goods during transit and preventing or limiting wastage and destruction
1351. Unity of peoples in different countries
1352. International cooperation and peace
1353. Charity organisations – giving shelter, scholarships, assistance;
1354. Aid agencies that help the poor
1355. Absence of calamities, plagues, natural disasters
1356. For the safety of those who escape natural disasters
1357. For work, employment and occupations
1358. For giving us work to do
1359. For receiving training to work
1360. For the opportunity to work
1361. For being able, healthy, and motivated to work
1362. For being employed at all
1363. For being employed legally
1364. For being employed productively
1365. For being happily employed
1366. For being paid for what we love to do[50]
1367. For being paid to work[51]
1368. For having a place to go to, called "Work" or office, rather than be idle
1369. For working in jobs with long term security whose services are essential[52]

---

[50] Most boys love to play football in childhood. Some are so good that they become professional footballers.

[51] We all need to work to eat, but slaves work for no pay at all.

[52] During the Coronavirus-induced lockdown, only essential services were permitted to operate: food chain supply,

medicines, visiting doctors, removing wastes, etc.

1370. For having a conducive environment to work in (the right room temperature)
1371. For receiving training and being qualified for work (training, graduation)
1372. For receiving training at work and gaining experience
1373. For having a vacancy to fill – by retirement or promotion
1374. For the availability of work (unemployment rates soar when vacancies are scarce)
1375. Having options of which job to take[53]
1376. Having equality at work[54]
1377. For the dignity of labour
1378. For jobs that pay us well enough to cater to our needs
1379. For the salary that we earn
1380. For getting paid promptly and regularly
1381. For being shortlisted for interviews[55] and for having referees who recommend us
1382. For success at job interviews or successful floating of private businesses
1383. For colleagues at work and cooperation
1384. For kind bosses, supervisors and line managers
1385. For giving us the grace to continue when work or boss is difficult
1386. For gadgets that help us discharge our duties properly
1387. For helping us to meet targets or work schedules
1388. For companies that do well and have good returns

---

[53] A brilliant doctor sat two interviews for a job in a matter of six days. He was offered a Consultant post in hospital A and a Senior Lecturer's position with clinical duties equivalent to a consultant's standing in the neighbouring teaching hospital. He mulled over the pros and cons before choosing the latter. Having a choice is a blessing.

[54] In times past, women and trade union groups had to fight for the right to vote, for equality.

[55] In the 1980s, a doctor in London said that he got ONE interview for every 25 applications he ever sent

1389. For companies whose products are essential for humanity or save lives
1390. For job satisfaction
1391. For periodic rest breaks at work and paid holidays
1392. For the success of the corporations who employ us
1393. For journey mercies to and from work
1394. For favors, awards, and promotions at work
1395. For workplace pension that provides for us after retirement
1396. **MARRIAGE** - the gift of the institution of marriage
1397. Helping opposite mates to attract
1398. Letting us grow old enough to marry
1399. Giving us a desire to marry
1400. Finding a partner
1401. Partner agreeing
1402. Not being jilted
1403. Obtaining parental approval and consent for spouse
1404. Not being duped into marriage[56]
1405. That I grew old enough to marry
1406. That I am blessed with the fruits of marriage that fill my house with joy
1407. The Wedding – a successful event
1408. Planning it
1409. Provision - Money for Wedding
1410. Having friends to help
1411. Having extra parents in the form of "in-laws."
1412. For the blessings of faithful and agreeable relatives-in-law
1413. Having people attend our wedding
1414. Receiving wedding presents
1415. Blessed with fine weather on the wedding day (no rains, etc.)
1416. Travel mercies for those attending[57]

---

[56] In two independent stories with the same theme, an Algerian and an Indian man sued their respective wives the day after their weddings. When each man saw his wife's face in natural light, they were unhappy with their facial blemishes and pimples. Each man claimed that he was duped into the marriage.

[57] A man in Abuja, Nigeria, refused to shake his friend's hand because he refused to honour his pledge to attend his Wedding. The spurned man explained

1417. No ill health on the wedding day (Some have cancer. Some are in a wheelchair for theirs).
1418. No fights
1419. Having no one to ruin it[58]
1420. No hitches in arrangements – cake, program, vicar, certificate,
1421. Chauffeur for the day.
1422. Having parents witness one's great day
1423. Groomsmen, Bridesmaids, caterers, helpers
1424. Honeymoon – site, experience, travel
1425. House safe while away for it
1426. Benefits of marriage - societal respect
1427. Companionship
1428. Helps
1429. Cooperation
1430. Sexual pleasure (having the urge and having it satisfied)
1431. Having erections
1432. Sustaining erection
1433. Pleasure of ejaculation
1434. For the enjoyment of orgasm (climax)
1435. The post coital somnolence
1436. Privacy
1437. Ready, willing, mate
1438. Healthy mate
1439. Pleasuring the spouse
1440. Pleasuring yourself
1441. Mate giving consent

---

that he had a road traffic accident on the way to the said wedding ceremony, was hospitalized for three months, and that he ought to be the One accusing the groom of not checking on his welfare!

[58] In 1973 in Ibadan, Nigeria, when the officiating priest announced, "If any man knows a cause why these two may not be joined in holy matrimony let him speak now ..." a woman stepped forward and said she was the legally married wife. She brought a framed photograph of their two children. That ended the wedding ceremony.

1442. Mate giving consent easily (without much coaxing or coercion)
1443. Having sex rather than being raped
1444. Not being discarded after sex
1445. Not being divorced after sex
1446. A safe home to raise kids
1447. For marrying and being allowed by parents-in-law to enjoy our marriage without

molestation – Sparkle R. 2006.[59]

1448. That children grow up under parental care.
1449. Help for orphans; the blessing of adopted and foster parents
1450. For those who chose not to marry – spared many troubles
1451. They are spared Sexually Transmitted Infections, bickering, nagging, arguments, and fights.
1452. For the privilege that our birth, family, birthplace or race confers on us
1453. The blessing of the Bible and written texts that provide marriage guidance
1454. God's word reaching us
1455. The Holy Spirit helps our understanding
1456. The Word of God is a lamp unto our feet; a light unto our paths
1457. The freedom of worship God in spirit and in truth
1458. Evangelists
1459. Pastors and other workers in the church
1460. The fellowship of brethren

---

[59] In the USA, a man fell in love with a workmate. His parents disapproved of the relationship. He married her anyway, and they moved away to Atlanta. She had a baby. One day, the wife was murdered while her husband was at work. The police couldn't solve the murder case until several years later when a witness to the murder informed police she knew the murderer. Bank statements showed he was paid shortly after the crime. The man who sent him was tracked down and interviewed. He confessed to having been asked to solicit for the murder – by the disgruntled father-in-law. It was established that he innocent bride was murdered for the sin of being in love.

1461. Missionaries and missionary work
1462. For every soul that answers the gospel call and finds salvation

Chapter 5 | SOCIAL, ENVIRONMENTAL, THE PHYSICAL WORLD

1463. For giving man language
1464. For the essentials and necessities of life
1465. **Water**, food, air, freedom, human rights
1466. For water to drink
1467. For clean, potable water[60]
1468. To water our fields, farms, and crops
1469. For washing and bathing
1470. For preparing our meals
1471. For hydro-electric power
1472. For the principles of floatation
1473. For the cleansing effect of water – flowing rivers wash away debris
1474. Rain run-off (erosion) carries away dirt
1475. Raindrops chisel away at rocks freeing up valuable minerals that enrich the soil.
1476. Oceans on which we can sail to reach other locations
1477. Oceans on which merchant ships sail to transport heavy goods
1478. Oceans which act as drainage receptacles for earth's waters
1479. The power of water, as we see in tsunamis[61]
1480. For volcanoes and their provision of soil nutrients
1481. And pumice mined from volcanic ash
1482. For the power that is bottled up in the earth's core as revealed by earthquakes

---

[60] In Chicago, USA, in 1902, Dr. Alice Hamilton discovered that typhoid was due to sewage seeping into water pipes.

[61] On March 11, 2011, a tsunami engulfed the east coast of Japan. Amongst the abiding memories was how the water lifted a ship onto the roof of a multi-story building, swept off numerous houses, and tossed many vans.

1483. For mountains which are the sources for water springs
1484. For providing us with a roof over our heads
1485. Keeping us safe in our homes – from the elements, beasts, burglars
1486. Ability to own our own homes or afford to rent accommodation
1487. Helping us to meet our mortgage obligations
1488. Preventing our homes from being washed away during storms
1489. For the universe and our solar system
1490. **The Sun**, moon, and the stars
1491. Energy from the sun, which gives us light to see,
1492. The beauty of the colorful rainbow, and,
1493. The promise of God that the rainbow conveys
1494. Sun's energy that warms up animals and humans
1495. The sun heats up our environment[62]
1496. Sun's energy that makes plants grow and makes our summer beautiful
1497. The sun's energy aids photosynthesis in plants by which we obtain food
1498. Sun's energy improves our health and improves our mood
1499. Its ultraviolet rays help our body to make vitamin D
1500. Vitamin D that improves our immunity and strengthens our bones
1501. Equipping our body with melanin to prevent radiation damage
1502. Sun's energy that we harness through Solar panels
1503. For the power of hurricanes, volcanoes, earthquakes, and thunderbolts
1504. For unseen forces in our lives: gravity, cohesion, adhesion, magnetism

---

[62] In winter, some cities have a foot of snowfall and subzero temperatures. Six months later, the weather is warm or hot in summer, and air-conditioners and fans are employed to cool. The amount of heat needed to melt the snow and heat up the world is massive!

1505. The energy that keeps us from being blown off by the fast-spinning earth[63]
1506. For the cyclicity, regularity, and predictability of weather patterns
1507. For the knowledge of the science to give the accurate weather forecast
1508. For the lives saved by following accurate forecast of adverse weather events
1509. For the gift of time.

1508 THE GIFT OF TIME #55

We thank God for the gift of time by which we measure our daily routines, life, work shifts, travel, growth, investment and others. Without the sun, we would have no time at all. A complete journey of our earth around the sun (revolution) gives us what we call a *year.* One rotation of our planet on its axis gives us a *day.* As we wake up each day, where we live on earth is being turned to face the sun. The turning (rotation) continues till noon, then, just before we are moved away from the glare of the sun, we say the sun is setting. The fact is that we are the one "setting," because the sun is constant in its position, suspended, as it were, upon nothing in space. But our planet earth is kept close to the sun by the gravitational pull of the sun. When our planet completely moves our location on the globe away from the sun, we say that darkness has fallen – night

---

[63] If you drop a tiny piece of paper on a fast-spinning globe or ball, it gets blown off. Our planet spins on its axis at the equator at a speed of 1,000 miles per hour (733mph at the north pole). Why do we not get blown off? The Lord makes us spin *at the same speed* with the fast-moving earth, so it appears as if we are static!

time. Our night however gives people on the opposite side of the globe to face the sun – so, it is morning to them. This is the reason that when countries on longitude zero (Greenwich Mean Time on the Prime Meridian) like the UK, France, Morocco and Ghana are waking up, those along longitude 180 degrees like New Zealand, are going to bed. This was the sense that poet John Ellerton tried to convey in 1870, in his hymn, *The Day Thou gavest, Lord, is ended.* In it, he wrote,

> *The sun that bids us rest is waking,*
> *Our brethren 'neath the western sky*

1504 BLOWN AWAY #56

We are moving at a breakneck speed every moment of the day, but we don't feel it.

A day of 24 hours is the measure of the time it takes our world to spin on its axis. The sun is in our solar system, and when the world turns our part of the world to the sun, we have daylight. At daybreak, only little rays shine through, then high noon, but as we moved away from the sun, we experience the sunset, then the darkness of night. At the point that London is basking in strong sunshine, Australia and New Zealand are in the dead of night. Twelve hours later, we swap positions.

As the earth's circumference at the equator is roughly 47,075 kilometers, and the world needs to cover this in 24 hours, the earth travels at nearly 2000 kilometers per hour or 1,250 miles per hour. (*To imagine how fast this is, it is twice as fast as a passenger jet. Stand safely well off a motorway as vehicles go past. In England, this is about*

70 miles per hour. It is frightening how each car whistles past. Imagine that speed 17 times faster. That's how fast the earth is spinning). Humans, buildings, towns turn with the ground at this unimaginable speed. But what keeps us from falling off, from being blown away into space?

First is gravity, the God-given force that attracts us, centripetally, to the core of the earth. More important, however, is that we are spinning *pari passu* with planet earth – together, in synchrony, at the same time. But to God be the glory, these movements do not affect, derail or disturb us. We are not blown away.

1510. For night and days,

1511. For various seasons and the beauty of each

1512. For trade winds that bring warmth and rain

1513. For the dew and the rain that water our soils

1514. For the cleansing property of rainfall – reducing dust and pollen

1515. For the tremendous relief of the rain after hot, dry weather

1516. For the abundance of fish in rivers, and revival of those that survive the dry spells yearly

1517. And the growth of grass for animal food

1518. For winds that help propel the sails of watercrafts

1519. For the cooling effect of breezes

1520. And winds that help the pollination of plants

1521. For mountains, seas and forests

1522. For natural resources

1523. For mineral resources like coal for heating, crude oil, natural gas

1524. For the technology and know-how to mine various minerals

1525. And the smith-skill to turn them to precious jewels

1526. For the beautiful jewelry that smiths fashion from precious stones

1527. For the wealth that mineral resources provide for countries where they are found
1528. For the richness of volcanic ash and plant nutrients from mountainsides
1529. Geographic features that beautify our world – landscapes, rolling mountains, meadows
1530. For the beautiful blue sky and clear ocean waters
1531. For sandy beaches and cool seaside breezes
1532. For the immense power in volcanic eruptions and the minerals deposited
1533. For the ozone layer protecting us from the sun's harmful rays
1534. For ancient civilizations – writings, legends, proverbs, parables
1535. For Technological advances and the increase in knowledge
1536. For man's intelligence and creativity
1537. For education, instruction, teachers, and institutions of learning
1538. For engineering, engineering feats and machines that aid our daily work
1539. For the law-enforcement personnel and police that are not murderous or corrupt
1540. For officers of military installations and all the security apparatus of each country

1541. **Inventions**, various inventions
1542. For all mechanisms that make life easy to live: electricity,
1543. Water cisterns and modern toilet facility, the electric light bulb, vacuum flask
1544. Telephones, cables, telegrams
1545. Courier services
1546. The multiple functions of a smartphone
1547. The manufacture of kitchen appliances
1548. The convenience that kitchen appliances bring
1549. The blessings of Food Technology.

1535 INCREASE IN KNOWLEDGE – TECHNOLOGY #57

In its basic form, the average kitchen has benefitted from the introduction of technological aids: appliances like the microwave, blender, cooker, fridge, and dishwasher have cut down on old drudgery. Growing up in Ikole-Ekiti, bringing water up to the boil for my dad's morning bath, or cooking the evening meal when my mother delegated it to me, was laborious. We used firewood that had been sourced from dried fallen logs in the woods. We carried these on our heads for up to a mile or two. Then, strong boys used an axe to split the big logs into pieces, about 6 x 36 inches. A typical cooking session started with lighting the wood with a live ember and fanning it into flame. That caused the eyes to water and go red from smoke irritation with a lot of coughing from the carbon gases. Such fires needed close attention and the time that it took to cook any food depends of the attention given. However, today, we have convenient electric and gas cookers.

In those days, the roasting sun heats up everything that was exposed to it, including stored water. To cool our drinking water, we stored spring water in large earthen pots kept in dark rooms, whereas we now have refrigerators. Food off the pot was fairly hot, and certain types of meals needed to be eaten when hot or warm but some would be lukewarm or cold before they were served to the household or to party guests. Our evening meal – supper – was the main meal of the day and frequently was a dumpling of pounded (mashed) yam or yam flour, *amala*. Dumplings are best-eaten piping hot hence our mothers would serve their husbands' portions wrapped leaves or plastic bags, napkins or sheets of clothes to keep them warm. Much later we had vacuum warmers. Today we have the microwave oven. Certain food items can now be cooked and canned or stored in a deep freezer. We had to grind spices like dried melon seeds, hot chili pepper, and locust beans on flat stone slabs, and now we have blenders. Corn that used to be pounded in mortars with pestles can now be milled. I grew up to see my dapper senior brothers ironing their *starched* khaki school uniforms with a hot coal-heated pressing iron but these have been replaced by the electric iron. Water used to be boiled in pots and tea brewed in teapots with spouts, but today we have electric kettles, coffee filters, and *Thermos* flasks. Food technology used to be problematic and hazardous but today, the refrigerator and the freezer have improved storage and arguably, reduced diarrhoeal diseases from food poisoning.

In 2000, being the turn of the millennium, my son's high school held their annual essay competition for pupils in the junior school (years 7-9, the first three years in a secondary school). The school invited students to write an essay on what they considered to be the two most significant inventions of the twentieth-century. Tolu chose '*The discovery of the World Wide Web (Internet)*' and '*The discovery of Penicillin.*' We know how Penicillin and other antimicrobials have revolutionised medicine and reduced deaths from common infections like syphilis, staphylococcal infections, pneumonia, and tuberculosis. The explosion in the use of the internet has been astounding in communications, finance, and videography. Useful sites and applications such as *Wikipedia, Google, Facebook, WhatsApp,* electronic mail, *LinkedIn*, and *Zoom* meetings are now household names. It might be safe to say that they have become part and parcel of daily living. My smartphone can perform various functions that incorporated multiple trades that were offered outdoors some thirty years ago: photography, telephone services, diary-keeping, note-taking, Filofax, photocopying, postal services, map reading, A-Z maps of British cities, booking of flights, trains, and hotels; diary, calendars, bookshelves for my collections of British Encyclopaedia, reference books, dictionaries and banking services. Man has gone to the moon, and satellite navigation has improved telecommunications immensely. *Youtube* has become a home-based but ubiquitous, effective audiovisual private teacher. In medicine, keyhole surgery has improved patient turn-over, as has robotics. These have shortened the time spent in hospitals, saved money and freed up time for productivity. One can only imagine where we would be in twenty years. It is not for nothing that the Bible told us, *"But as for you, Daniel, conceal these words and seal up the scroll until the end of time. Many will run to and fro, and knowledge shall increase." (Daniel 12:4).*

1550. The multiple functions of the smartphone – contacts, appointment calendar,
   reminders, alarms, photos, camera, calculator, telephone receiver, emailing, etc.,
1551. Telecommunications, wireless radio, television, internet
1552. Photography that records important faces; Writing, Printing, Drama, Arts,
1553. The invention of computers, batteries, solar energy, power generating plants
1554. Clothing, garments, central heating, air conditioning technology
1555. Music, music recordings, storage, and reproduction
1556. Various forms of vehicles: land, sea, rail, air
1557. For travel, its planning and the relative safety we enjoy
1558. Travel – Road journeys. Good road conditions
1559. Safety when driving
1560. Guiding us unerringly when we do not know our destinations
1561. Helping us to avoid accidents (some wheels come off, tires burst, cars veer off roads).
1562. Efficient train services – promptness and reliability
1563. Helping our trains not to derail
1564. Providing electricity to power trains
1565. Ability to change railway tracks smoothly
1566. The heavy cargo that trains transport
1567. Train drivers who can stay awake on long journeys
1568. Waterways: buoyancy and floatation of ships: preventing sinking
1569. Guidance to navigate high seas with no landmarks for direction
1570. Calm sailing conditions, reducing the strength of destructive waves

1571. Ability to avoid rocks and cliffs
1572. Holiday cruises, the crew, the staff, the catering, board, and success of cruises
1573. The invention of planes
1574. The power that keeps planes suspended in the skies
1575. Accurate navigation above the clouds
1576. Functioning equipment; autopilot capabilities
1577. Relatively safe travel conditions, virtually no mid-air collisions;
1578. Smooth checking in and prompt schedules when traveling
1579. Pilots and cabin crew on whose know-how our lives depend in mid-air
1580. Maintenance of cabin pressure
1581. Successful deployment of landing gears and wheels
1582. Providing clear landing weather and space for aircrafts
1583. Granting successful landing when planes are in distress or engines fail
1584. Medical discoveries – causes of diseases, treatments, surgical operations,
1585. Advanced techniques – care of premature babies, organ transplants,
1586. Keyhole surgery, antiseptics, antibiotics, anaesthesia
1587. The gift of the universal language of laughter to peoples of the world
1588. And the gift of merry-making with dancing
1589. And music
1590. The gift of language to communicate effectively
1591. Giving diverse languages to diverse peoples
1592. The ability for outsiders to learn languages of other peoples
1593. **THE LITTLE THINGS OF LIFE:** Seeing the moon (vide supra), not stepping on my glasses when I've misplaced them, finding my lost car keys or house keys; being allowed to go away scot free when a policeman had stopped me without charging me.

Chapter 6 | ANIMALS

1594. For creating animals – for food, company, help and other uses
1595. Giving us dominion over animals and the ability to control or tame them
1596. For horses, we use for transport and sports,
1597. For dogs that we use for companionship, hunting, blind guides, sentry and sniffing
1598. For cats, we keep as pets
1599. For poultry that give us eggs and chicken meat
1600. For cattle that provide us with milk, beef, and butter
1601. For goats that give us cheese
1602. For sheep that provide us with wool
1603. For camels that help our desert journeys and haulage of goods;
1604. For whales that give us whale oil
1605. For creating food chains and making us (humans) the apex predators
1606. For eliminating sick, feeble, old, dying, and dead animals
1607. For giving man the wisdom to be able to control all animals
1608. The ecosystem and the interdependence of animals
1609. Reproduction in animals – delicate, miraculous
1610. For the ability of certain animals to survive extreme climatic conditions
1611. The presence of the baculum in animals like the elephant
1612. The clearance of carrion from our environment by scavengers[64]
1613. For the clearance of vegetation and vegetable matter by saprophytic bacteria

---

[64] We possibly hate hyenas, vultures, and dung-beetles, but they clean up our environment by eating away carcasses, carrion, and droppings. Others include crabs, lobsters and jackals.

1614. The instinct for herbivores to consume placenta when their young are born

1614 HERBIVORES EATING FLESH #58

Scientists may classify animals based on the presence of the backbone (vertebra), what they eat, where they live, and how their babies are born and fed or suckled.

If we employed their nutrition, we have three groups: carnivores, herbivores, and omnivores. Big cats such as lions mainly feed on flesh, whereas hoofed animals eat vegetation. Man, bear, pig, sloths, mice, chimpanzees, dogs, chickens, turtles, piranhas, and catfish eat both flesh and vegetation. However, plant-eating animals are not strict or obligate herbivores because, at least once in their lifetime, these *vegetarians* eat meat for mainly scientific and survival reasons. When a calf is born to a zebra in the savannahs of Africa, the new mother eats up the placenta and licks the calf clean. This flesh-eating habit serves two purposes. The first is that the placenta, along with the blood that is shed at birth, may attract predators that can sniff the smell of blood or flesh from afar. To protect the newborn, the mother instinctively removes the source of unwanted attraction. In addition, these new calves tend to get to their feet in a matter of minutes. Otherwise, they are prey to hungry cats.

The second reason is that animals, unlike humans, cannot take oral iron tablets or receive a blood transfusion to offset whatever blood they lose during birthing processes. Women do bleed to death at the time of giving birth – indeed, excessive blood loss is the commonest cause of maternal deaths in pregnancy in the developing countries on earth. As of 2020, one woman was dying every two minutes from obstetric complications, three-fifths (60%) of which are due to bleeding. This is a marked improvement from the early noughties when the World Health Organisation introduced the *Millennium Development Goal, MGDs* initiative to address the world's health concerns. MDG #4 was aimed at reducing maternal mortality worldwide. Twelve years previously, in 2008, in those low-resourced countries, one woman was dying every minute chiefly from blood loss, abortion, miscarriage, eclampsia and infections. In most developed countries, the leading causes of maternal deaths were thromboembolic disease (blood clots), hypertensive disorders during pregnancy and ectopic pregnancy. All women in the hospitals have recourse to medical care, including being given haematinics (blood-building medicines) and blood transfusion for acute, life-threatening bleeding. In contrast, a giraffe, zebra, or wildebeest in the *Serengeti* is not so blessed. Eating their placenta is nature's way to replenish their stores of iron.

God, in His mercy, gave these animals the innate ability to eat the placenta that they shed. The placenta is a soft tissue that is laden with blood, and therefore high-quality iron storage. In other words, the blood "lost" in a placenta is recycled. The animal digests it and breaks it down to high-quality protein and iron, which its bones will utilise to make new blood cells. It means that each ungulate has the enzyme to digest the fleshy placenta, although their enzymes are mostly those that can digest vegetation. Plants are generally poor sources of proteins, but flesh is a rich source of first-class proteins. For all these intricate abilities and processes, I give praise to God.

1615. Fishes that supply us with food and provide commerce
1616. Birds that sing
1617. Birds that we eat for food (fowl, turkey, grouse, ducks)
1618. Birds that provide eggs for our food,

1619. For honey produced by bees
1620. For insects that pollinate flowers to make our crops bear fruits
1621. For the lessons man learns from animals and small organisms – industry by bees, organisation by ants, resilience by termites
1622. For the maternal instincts in animals, birds and certain fishes and crocodiles
1623. For the navigational instinct in migrating animals – elephants, pacific turtles, birds
1624. The ability of organisms that grow and survive in extreme temperatures

1624 ANIMALS IN EXTREME AND COLD TEMPERATURES (59)

Some biologists and naturalists usually tell us that organisms that live in frigid climates have adapted over time. They also claimed that the polar bear, the arctic fox, the penguin, the arctic vole, and so on, have evolved over centuries until they could survive and thrive in these hostile conditions. However, it is easy to see through these lies and the denial of the creative intelligence of the Almighty.

If these animals evolved and were able to adapt and survive, **how then did their ancestors who did not have the luxury of the time needed to adapt and evolve cope with the freezing conditions?** Why didn't they perish in the ice/snow? If they were not created purposefully to live in those harsh conditions and come ALREADY equipped with all the adaptations they would need, then surely, they would have been frozen to death before they had had time to evolve and adapt? These animals could not have migrated from a warm climate where conditions were ideal. Their systems, their heat-regulating mechanisms could not have withstood the sudden drop in temperature. Otherwise, we have to ask, "When these migrating birds and animals arrived in the Arctic and Antarctica, how did they survive, being unprepared? They would and ought to have been wiped out by the freezing conditions. They even managed to have cubs, chicks, and eggs that did not freeze! How was that possible?

We have to agree that they could not have survived, and therefore, there was no adaptation at all. God made them for those places and gave them the capacity, *ab initio*, to survive. That is an act of God, and we should praise God for His creative powers and intelligence rather than give this glory to "evolution."

1621 INSECT LESSONS #60

All social insects share similar characteristics of industry, assiduity, tenacity and unity. On a summer day, honey bees would have started collecting pollen grains as soon as the day breaks and continue till it gets dark. If a bee finds pollen, it alerts the hive, and leads its companions to the source.

Termites work together to build their hills and, without the benefit of a president, parliament, legislature, or cabinet, they choose a queen termite that they feed, nurture, and respect. No other bee competes with the queen. In return, the queen sacrifices her freedom, aesthetics and life to become an egg-laying automaton. From this egg factory, thousands of termites would emerge from the larvae. These eggs are well tended by workers and as soon as they are old enough, the newborns join the adult workforce as soldiers or foragers for food. When they fight, none is found slacking. If their habitat is destroyed, they do not feel sorry for themselves, rather, they rally, regroup and set about to work flat out to repair any damage, sometimes, to rebuild a structure that may grow up to five feet above ground level.

Ants are usually referred to as the epitome of industry. Everything written above about the bee and the termite applies to the ant. Like bees and termites, ants do not wait for any captain or general to assign work to them. They sometimes carry leaves that are several times their weight or size. In South America, some tailor ants do cross fast flowing rivers! Their ingenuity is impressive. One ant plants its feet on the bank, and another walks over it to be joined to it end-to-end. This process continues until they span the river. The others then use these as bridges to crawl across the river, and one by one, they dismount. Needless to say, some of these selfless ants will be washed away. It is the price for co-operation. The Bible rightly invites a lazy man to go and study the ant:

> *Go to the ant, you sluggard!*
> *Consider her ways and be wise,*
> *Which, having no captain,*
> *Overseer or ruler,*
> *Provides her supplies in the summer,*
> *And gathers her food in the harvest*
> *How long will you slumber, O sluggard?*
> *(Proverbs 6:6-8, NKJV)*

The lessons are:
1. Ants are orderly and organized.
2. Diligent and hardworking.
3. They work in collaboration – there is no selfish ant. Team work is excellent.

4. They work as equals, none lords it over the other, and none cheats the commonwealth.
5. The ant rises early to work, does not oversleep or laze idly in bed;
6. It has foresight and prepares for the rainy day
7. It does not waste opportunity or procrastinate; it seizes the moment;
8. It plans for the future, making hay when the sun is shining. It might also be the equivalent of a man planning for his old age by putting away savings or paying into a pension scheme or investing in land or property. Only a foolish man spends all that he earns because when earning days are over, he will starve and become a beggar. The ant never begs. Notice too that both sexes work for the good of the colony.

Chapter 7 | PLANTS

1625. Giving us plants – the variety of plants: diversity, colour, beauty
1626. Giving us plants for food – roots (potato), stems (sugar cane), leaves, fruits, seeds
1627. For plants that we use for oil: coconut, palm, olive
1628. For oils that we use for cosmetics and drugs.
1629. For giving us plants for furniture
1630. For plants that provide shade from the hot tropical sun
1631. For plants that provide us with fuel for cooking, and heating
1632. For coal derived from fossil plants of years gone by
1633. For plants that provide fabric materials for clothing (cotton, raffia)
1634. Plants that we use for medicine (cinchona, willow, coca)
1635. For plants, we use for beverages (tea, coffee, cocoa)
1636. For drinks that come from plants, such as fruit juice, fruit smoothies, and wine.
1637. For the gift of Agriculture (and other arts, crafts, and professions)
1638. For making plants to regrow after wildfires
1639. And for reviving various plants after prolonged droughts
1640. Plants whose flowers beautify our gardens.
1641. The aroma of fresh plants and flowers in the countryside,
1642. For the vitamins that humans derive from plants – fruits, tubers, leaves, grains
1643. For paper and pulp from plants
1644. For rubber used in tire-making, gum, and elastics
1645. For fiber such as cotton for clothing
1646. For dyes for that beautify clothing
1647. Dyes that we use as ink for writing
1648. For plant wood - furniture, canoes, fuel,
1649. For containers, we fashion out of plants – baskets, boxes, cups, gourds,

1650. Plants remove carbon dioxide from our air and release oxygen
1651. For the process of photosynthesis by which our food is stored in roots and leaves
1652. For making the smoke emitted by firewood to be non-toxic otherwise, our poor womenfolk who use these for cooking would die in their kitchens.
1653. For the ability of plants to prevent soil erosion
1654. Plants and planks used for building houses and sheds
1655. For tall plants that act as storm and windshields for our homes and buildings
1656. Plants provide food for animals; and,
1657. Shelter for arboreal wild animals and birds.
1658. For growth rings that help us to determine the age of trees
1659. Deadwood on which wild mushrooms grow
1660. Deadwood that provides shelter for larvae and caterpillars
1661. Plants – provide jobs for those who tend them (Foresters, loggers, craftsmen).
1662. Plants that offer recreation and pastime for gardeners;
1663. For the way our soil is fertilized naturally by dead plants and animal wastes
1664. For giving man the knowledge of cultivating crops
1665. For the interdependence of all of creation on one another – symbiosis, commensalism
1666. For the medicinal properties of plants – such as aspirin, caffeine, theophylline, digitalis, codeine, morphine, atropine, camphor, quinine, etc.
1667. For the knowledge of man in discovering the medicinal properties of plants
1668. Plant parts we use for recreation: cricket and polo bats, conker seeds, ayo seeds
1669. For the beauty of flowers with assorted colors
1670. For flowers that practise nyctinasty – the ability to react to light and close up at night. These are called "daybloomers" and protect their pollen from "night robbers!"
1671. We praise God than man and scientists, and even Charles Darwin didn't know why some plants are day-bloomers. (e.g., Four-O-Clocks, Dandelions, Tulips, Poppy, Crocuses), and

some are active only at night (Evening primrose, Gladiolus; Queen of the Night). Similarly, man does not yet know why some plants and flowers shut up their petals or leaves when a man or an animal touches them. (*Nyctinasty: Greek: Linux = night; Bastos = pressed down*).

1672. **Finally**, we praise God for the things of life that we cannot see but which we know exist because we can see their effects, for example, wind, emotion, heat, electricity, microwave energy, and so forth. Similarly, we cannot see God, but we can see His hand in nature and see and feel His influence. God exists. He is invisible but very much present with us.

1673. For giving us the grace to believe without having seen – to "believe in faith."

1674. And for giving us the heart of praise for all of the above.

1625 THE BLESSING OF PLANTS (61)

As humans, we depend primarily on plants for our needs and survival. They provide most of our food, medicines, building materials and furniture. Cotton is a vital clothing fibre. The atmospheric air we breathe in is purified daily by plants that extract carbon dioxide and replace it with oxygen. Carbon dioxide is the waste product of our respiration. At the same time, oxygen is the waste product of photosynthesis, the process by which plants convert the sun's energy into starch. Thus, we have a symbiotic relationship with plants.

I was taught at Edinburgh university that the amount of fat consumed by individuals is directly proportional to their nation's wealth. When I was growing up, Nigeria was not yet classified as a prosperous country – certainly not in the villages. Kids like me would hunt the bushes for rodents, squirrels, fish and crabs. Strong palm stems were used to construct bridges over streams; the fronds were used for making brooms, the bark of the midvein of the frond would be woven into baskets. The midveins nearest to the axil of the frond are usually devoid of leaves and, as they have tapered ends, they make for toothpicks.

The array of medicines obtained from plants is impressive. Aspirin is obtained from the bark of the willow tree and is used for pain relief, fever and the prevention of blood clotting. Cocaine is a compound isolated from the coca plant. Ancient Peruvian farm workers chewed the leaves to pep up their energy. It is used for pain relief in medical practice. Digitalis works by slowing down the rate of the human heartbeat and increases the force of heart contractions. It is commonly used in the treatment of heart failure. It is derived from the Foxglove plant. From the Opium Poppy comes opiates such as morphine that is a staple pain relief medication during childbirth. A less potent form of morphine is codeine which doubles up as an analgesic and cough relief. Both can constipate and can be added to a formulation called *kaolin et morph* as a remedy for childhood diarrhoea. Various tribes worldwide use diverse roots, leaves and barks for treating fevers, infections, infestations and other maladies.

.

DO PRAYERS AND PRAISING GOD GIVE US OUR REQUESTS? #62

The emphatic message is this, 'Lord, teach us how to pray.' The Bible also says that "it is good to praise the Lord." The Lord Jesus Christ encouraged us to make our requests known to God and that he who asks, receives. However, when we have prayed, we sometimes arrogate to ourselves the glory that should be God's by saying that we received things from God BECAUSE we prayed! Wow! Never in a million years. It is not because we prayed but because of God's mercy, grace and providence. That is the reason He makes the sunshine to shine, and the rain to fall, on the Just and the Unjust. He allows some people – unbelievers – to be fabulously wealthy whereas, some people pray fervently and sincerely to barely scrape a living. The richest man on planet earth was never a Christian. Mansa Musa of the ancient Mali Empire was said to be a trillionaire in his day. Yet, John the Baptist was poor by earthly standards. Despite all of these, Christ had this to say about John in Luke7:28, "Amongst those born of women, there is not a greater prophet than John the Baptist..." By God's and Heaven's reckoning, John the Baptist was the greatest human product that ever lived. King Solomon before him was the richest king; today's technological giants like Bill Gates, Joseph Bezos, and Mark Zuckerberg are rich but not as great as these two biblical figures. There are wealthy sheiks in Arabia, and it is reasonably safe to suggest that none of these pray or believe like John nor pray in Jesus' name.

Final Thoughts: Knowledge, of Man and God 63

In this final note, I reflect on an amazing feature of our contemporary lives.

The study of dendrochronology – the science that deals with studying the annual growth rings of trees in determining the dates and time sequence of past events – shows us how objects like trees can be a diary of world events! On the cut surface of a tree trunk, scientists can tell when a forest fire occurred because a crescentic dark scar will represent the event amidst the brown pulp of the tree. The yearly growth of the tree is represented by concentric rings – one ring for each year of existence. Similar objects sometimes store up information for men, such as fossils, stomach contents, bones, radioactive carbon, rock strata and a few others.

In criminology, the world has come in leaps and bounds from when suspected witches were hanged or burnt on mere accusation, to careful scientific evaluation of facts surrounding charges and accusations. Both prosecution and defense lawyers employ these. Even now, there are complicated cases where the evidence of guilt is so persuasive and leads to a penal sentence. Still, in many instances, justice had been misplaced, as in the case of Patricia Starling (note 32, p89 above). Several people have been put to death by the state only for newer evidence to surface and prove the innocence of a convicted or slain person thus creating a double dilemma of the wrongful man being convicted and the guilty man still on the loose in public to either continue to wreak havoc or enjoy a freedom that he did not deserve.

Many unsolved cases are now being successfully cleared because of further scientific advances. In the past, prosecutors employed the blood grouping of an accused to establish guilt or innocence. However, because blood groups are relatively few and many people share the same antigens this makes this method of convicting an accused unreliable. The Human Leucocyte Antigen was next employed, but this too gave way to fingerprints. Fingerprints are mostly unique to individuals, but it is not infallible. The person matching the print may err as FOUR scientists did when they erroneously linked Brandon Mayfield to the Madrid train bombing in 2004. It was later that the real culprit was identified. Today, retinal eye display and voice recognition technology are so trusted to be unique to each of us that they are used at passport controls at Customs in airports and personal identifications to access bank accounts, respectively. It is likely that in the future, we will discover more characteristics that are unique to the person. As at today, it is marvelous that each of the 7.5 billion people on earth, and perhaps all who lived before us, has or have had at least one feature that was unique to the individual. That takes some crafting by a superior, intelligent God.

Space is yet to be fully explored. The moon is perhaps conquered, but Mars and more distant planets are waiting. This sun is yet to be understood, as are the Stars, the Black Hole, and the belly of the earth. There are yet more wonders of nature. We cannot get to the earth's core, where temperatures are reputed to be hotter than the sun. Such things as the metal composition of earth's body can only be deduced by experiment and extrapolations, but for those who know, believe in, and trust God, there is One who knows! He allows us to know just what is enough for us and the rest He keeps to Himself (Deuteronomy 29:29).

For the things we know, for the things we don't, for God who created all things, for our uniqueness, and for the science that continues to educate us, I encourage you to join me as we praise the Lord.

In closing, permit me to reiterate, reader, the above passage in Deuteronomy because it reassures us that we will not necessarily discover all the answers we seek on earth. God allows us to know just what is enough for us, and He invites us to trust Him with the rest. Some things are secret, and He only has the answers. Jesus Christ explained that we are blessed if and when we believe without insisting on seeing – because God is good, trustworthy, and reliable.

The things of God are not like an arithmetical equation where two plus two equals four. With so many *unknown unknowns* around us, God calls us out in faith.

Let us trust Him. Let us believe in His providence. Let us count on His unfailing love. Come, let us fall before Him in worship, in faith, in believing in Jesus Christ, whom He sent into this world of sin to save us. If you have not been truly born again as Christ told Nicodemus in John 3:3, please, speak to God as you talk to a friend; confess your past, ask for His forgiveness, invite Christ to be the Lord of your life and start praising Him. Then get a copy of the Bible and read of God's excellent dealings with the children of men. It is nice to seek a Bible-believing church for fellowship. Iron sharpens iron.

How do we praise the Lord? by simply telling Him how grateful we are, much like when we thank our friends when they give us presents, or when a waiter serves us our food. Sometimes a chef cooks a nice meal that we enjoy, and we express our satisfaction to them, praising their skills. Occasionally, we send a 'Thank You card' to somebody who has done us some favour, and we tell our friends of their good deeds. Sometimes we give presents back to the person who has blessed us. Sometimes when we are surprised by somebody's generosity, we dance and jump in excitement.

These, precisely, are what we ought to do to God to show our appreciation: we may thank Him in our own words; we may dance, jump for joy or sing little songs of praise. We could give out little gifts or monetary donations to those we consider less fortunate than us. Howsoever we do it, we must be sincere and speak from the heart, and ultimately be able to say with the Psalmist,

LET EVERYTHING THAT HAS BREATH PRAISE THE LORD. Psalm 150:6.

Lightning Source UK Ltd.
Milton Keynes UK
UKHW021845040722
405350UK00009B/1663

9 781911 697213